Nita Mehta's
THAI
cooking for the Indian kitchen

Nita Mehta's
THAI
cooking for the Indian kitchen

100% TRIED & TESTED RECIPES

Nita Mehta

B.Sc. (Home Science), M.Sc. (Food and Nutrition)
Gold Medalist

Tanya Mehta

SNAB
Publishers Pvt. Ltd.

Nita Mehta's
THAI

cooking for the Indian kitchen

2nd Print 2007

ISBN 81-7869-081-0

Food Styling & Photography: Tanya Mehta

Layout and laser typesetting:

National Information
Technology Academy
3A/3, Asaf Ali Road
New Delhi-110002
N.I.T.A.
☎ 23252948

Picture on cover:	Thai Red Curry
	Masaman Curried Rice
Picture on page 1:	Crispy Vegetables
	Thai Flat Noodles with Peanuts
Picture on page 2-3:	Spring Rolls, Crispy Chicken in Shell
	Crunchy Salad with Rice Flakes
Picture on page 4:	Orient Noodle Soup
	Chicken & Coconut Soup
Picture on page 94:	Thai Chicken Satay
Picture on backcover:	Batter Fried Prawns in Lemon Sauce

Published by:

SNAB
Publishers Pvt Ltd
3A/3 Asaf Ali Road
New Delhi-110002
Tel:23250091, 23252948
Telefax:.91-11-23250091

The Best of Cookery Books

Editorial and Marketing office:
E-159, Greater Kailash-II, N.Delhi-110048
Tel: 91-11-29214011, 29218727, 29218574
Fax: 91-11-29225218, 29229558
E-Mail: nitamehta@email.com
     nitamehta@nitamehta.com

Website: http://www.nitamehta.com
Website: http://www.snabindia's

Contributing Writers :
Anurag Mehta
Subhash Mehta

Editorial & Proofreading :
Rakesh
Ramesh

Printed at:
BRIJBASI ART PRESS LTD

Distributed by:
THE VARIETY BOOK DEPOT
A.V.G. Bhavan, M 3 Con Circus
New Delhi - 110 001
Tel: 23417175, 23412567; Fax: 23415335
E-mail: varietybookdepot@rediffmail.com

Price: Rs. 195/-

Introduction

*I*n Thailand, food is a celebration. For a Thai, cooking is a source of pride. Thai food is a combination of delicious aroma, brilliant colours and exotic spices. Thai cooking is simple, quick and healthy. It is particularly appealing because of its healthy, low fat method of cooking.

Thai cuisine is a confluence of Chinese, Malaya and Indian influence, which the Thai have skilfully adapted as distinctly their own. Try a traditional satay with peanut sauce, followed by red Thai curry and crispy vegetables with a tangy dipping sauce. Accompany these with Masaman Curried Rice or with Glass Noodles in sesame paste. Finish the meal with a wonderful dessert-Crispy Fried Ice-Cream ball.

Thai cooking involves exuberant use of chillies, lemon grass, ginger and coconut. As Thai food is considered spicy, we have mellowed it down with the minimum use of chillies. All the ingredients used in the recipes are easily available although their substitutes have been given in case of non-availability.

Discover the secrets of Thai cooking with this beautiful illustrated book. Follow the step by step instruction to make classic Thai meals in your own home.

Happy cooking!

Nita Mehta

About The Recipes

What's In A Cup?

INDIAN CUP
1 teacup = 200 ml liquid
AMERICAN CUP
1 cup = 240 ml liquid (8 oz)
The recipes in this book were tested with the Indian teacup which holds 200 ml liquid.

Contents

SOUPS   20

SALADS   30

SNACKS WITH DIPS   35

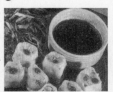

VEGETABLE CURRIES   49

VEG STIR FRIES   60

CHICKEN CURRIES 'N' STIR FRIES   64

FISH 'N' PRAWNS   74

NOODLES 'N' RICE   81

DESSERTS   88

Glossary of Indian Names/Terms   91

Ingredients used in Thai food

Basil: It belongs to the 'tulsi' family. It is available in dried form or as fresh basil leaves which are packed and sold by some vegetable vendors. Dried herbs are more concentrated so substitute 1 -2 tsp for ¼ cup of fresh basil leaves. The young, tender leaves of tulsi which is called the Holy basil, can be substituted for this sweet basil, but since they are much stronger than the real sweet basil, the leaves of this holy basil should be used sparingly in the recipe.

What is the best way to store basil mint?

Once I put basil leaves in a bowl of water thinking they would remain fresh and green. To my disappointment, they turned black! Then I discovered that standing basil in a glass of water with the leaves above the water, kept them fresh and green for a few days. During winters, you can keep this pretty bouquet on the kitchen counter and in summers keep the basil in the glass in the fridge.

Grow your own basil in pots!
Basil seeds grow into beautiful plants put into a pot.

Lemon grass : It is a common ingredient in Thai cuisine. The flavour of lemon grass is similar to that of lemon, yet it has its very own unique and haunting piquancy. To use, discard the bottom 1" of the stalk and peel some of the outer leaves. Chop the stalk and use it in curry pastes. The upper grass like portion is not edible and so it is added to dishes like soups, rice and curries to flavour them but removed from the dish before serving. Lemon grass will keep well for about 1-2 weeks in the fridge. Use 1-2 stalks per dish.

Lemon Rind: In absence of lemon grass, lemon rind makes a good substitute. To get lemon rind, grate a firm, fresh lemon on the finest holes of the grater without applying pressure. Grate only the yellow outer skin without grating the white pith beneath it. Rind of 2 lemons would do good for a stalk of lemon grass.

Bean Curd or Tofu: Bean Curd or Tofu is prepared from soya bean milk and resembles the Indian Paneer in taste and looks. I have thus substituted it with paneer to give you a few exciting delicacies.

Seasoning Cube & Veg Stock: Veg stock is an important agent for most soup and sauces. However, if you do not have stock ready or feel lazy to make a stock, you can use seasoning cubes mixed in water instead. Seasoning cubes are available as small packets.

These are very salty, so taste the dish after adding the cube before you put more salt. Always crush the seasoning cube to a powder before using it.

Dry Red Chilli: Dry Kashmiri red chillies are mainly used, as they impart a bright red colour to the dish without making it too hot. You can use regular dry red chillies also. They are mainly used in curries.

Coconut cream and milk: It is the liquid extracted from coconut flesh. Coconut cream is the liquid extracted from the first pressing. Coconut cream is the thickest and most concentrated extract. Coconut milk is the product of the second and third pressing and is much thinner.

Coconut milk is used in curries, while coconut cream is used mainly in desserts. Coconut cream is available in tetra packs or cans and can be diluted with water to make coconut milk. Coconut milk powder which is available can be mixed with some water to make coconut milk. The recipe at the end of this book is very easy to follow.

Bean Sprouts: These are shoots of moong beans or soya beans. The texture is crisp. To make bean sprouts at home, soak ½ cup of green beans (saboot moong dal) for about 8 hours. Discard water and tie in a muslin cloth. Keep them tied for 2-3 days, remembering to wet the cloth each day. When the shoots are long enough, wash carefully in water. Fresh bean sprouts will keep for 3-4 days if refrigerated in a perforated plastic bag.

Ginger/Galangal: Galangal' ginger is most commonly used in Thai cooking. The Thais use a wide variety of different 'gingers' in their cooking, all of which have subtle differences. As we do not have all the varieties in India, use regular ginger instead. Choose a very young or fresh ginger as it has a milder flavour. A good indication of young ginger is that the skin should be thin, soft and pale in colour.

Kaffir lime leaves (nimbu ke patte): These have a distinctive flavour and perfume.

The leaves are available dried, frozen or fresh from Oriental food shops and some greengrocers. If kaffir lime leaves are unavailable, any leaves of an Indian lemon tree or a plant would do. In this book we have not specified the use of kaffir limes for lime juice, but for a true Thai flavour use it whenever possible.

Tamarind (imli): This is the large pod of the tamarind tree. To use, soak the pulp in water, then strain and use as directed in the recipe.

The usual dilution is three parts water to one part tamarind. Tamarind is easily available. If unavailable, use a mixture of lime or lemon juice and treacle as a substitute.

Black Bean Sauce: This sauce is made from fermented black beans and has a pungent and salty flavour. It cannot be made at home. It is available ready made in bottles, at most leading stores (shops).

Soya Sauce: There are 2 kinds. One is dark and the other is light. Both are used for seasoning all foods. It cannot be made at home. It is available ready made in bottles, at most leading stores (shops).

Noodles:
Thin noodles are preferred to thick ones. They are usually cooked in boiling water till just done for about 1 minute only. Never overcook noodles as they turn thick on over cooking. They are cooked to a crisp tender stage.

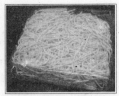

Rice Noodles: These extremely thin noodles resemble long, translucent white hair. Rice noodles are just soaked in hot water for 10 minutes and then drained before use. When deep fried they explode dramatically into a tangle of airy, crunchy strands that are used for garnish. The thin noodles are called **glass noodles**. In the absence of these, the regular noodles or rice seviyaan can be used.

Flat Noodles: These are also rice noodles, the only difference being they are flatter and wider to look. In absence of these, use flat pasta (fettucine).

Rice: Rice is the central dish of any Thai meal and the other dishes are considered to be side dishes.

Jasmine rice: For an authentic Thai meal serve steamed jasmine rice - cooked without salt. Jasmine rice is also called Thai fragrant rice and as its name suggests is delicately scented. You can use regular basmati rice also instead of it.

White glutinous rice/Sticky Rice: This rice can either be long or short grained and is sometimes called sweet or sticky rice. For savoury dishes, Thai cooks would use the long grain variety. Glutinous rice is very high in starch content, the cooked grains cling together in a mass and are soft and sticky. Short grain white glutinous rice is mainly used for desserts. You can use any ordinary quality rice for this.

Rice flour: Ready-made rice flour is easily available in market. To make it at home, grind raw rice (kachcha chaawal) to a smooth powder. Sift through a sieve (channi) to get a fine powder.

Spring Onions (hara pyaz): These are sometimes called scallions or green onions. In absence of it you can substitute it with regular onion. The green part is also used & should be added at the end.

Brown Sugar: Although the Thai use Palm Sugar in their cooking, brown sugar (which is easily available imparts almost the same flavour to the food is used instead.

Shallots/onions: These are smaller onions, lighter in colour and milder in flavour and belong to the onion family.

Star Anise *(Chakri Phool)***:** The dried, hard, brown, star shaped fruit has a fennel flavour. It is an important ingredient used in five spice powder. It can be substituted with saunf (fennel seeds).

Five Spice Powder: This mixture of five ground spices is slightly sweet and pungent. Roast together 2 tsp peppercorns (saboot kali mirch), 3 star anise (phool chakri), 6 cloves (laung), 4" stick cinnamon (dalchini), 3 tsp fennel (saunf). Grind all the ingredients of the powder in a small mixer to a powder. Strain the powder through a sieve (channi).

Carrot Flowers: *If the dish requires round slices of carrots, cut the carrot into round flowers instead. It enhances the look of stir fried dishes.*

For carrot flowers, peel a thick, big carrot. Cut into two pieces to get 2 shorter lengths. Firmly holding the carrot upright, with a small sharp knife, make 1/8 inch broad and deep lengthwise cuts along the length of the carrot. Tilt the knife slightly to take out the thin long piece from the cut to get a groove. Make 2-3 more grooves leaving equal space between them. Carefully, cut the carrot into round slices.

Spring Onion Flowers: To make spring onion flowers, cut off about ¼ inch piece from the white bulb end and leaving 3" from the bulb, cut off the greens. Slice the bulb thinly lengthwise till the end of the bulb. Now make similar cuts at right angles. Similarly for a green side, cut the green leaves with a pair of scissors, almost till the stem end to get thin strips. Place in iced water for some time until it opens up like a flower.

Carrot & Radish Tuberoses: *These look great when placed on the side of a salad, or next to the snacks on the serving platter. A sprig of green leaves of coriander, mint or parsley placed next to the flowers make them look prettier.*

Take a slender carrot or radish. Peel and wash it. Make a sharp angled cut, at about a height of 1½", about ½" downwards and inwards. Make 2 similar cuts from the remaining sides - all the cuts should meet at the end. Hold the top of the carrot with one

hand, and the base with the other. Twist the lower portion to break off the top portion. You will have a tuberose in one hand and the remaining part of the carrot in the other. Trim the left over carrot to get a pointed end. Make more flowers from the left over carrot. Keep them in ice-cold water for upto 3-4 days without getting spoilt. You can make such flowers with white radish (mooli) also.

Chilli Flower: *A chilli flower made from fresh red or green chilli is a wonderful garnish for a spicy dish.*

Choose a slightly thick chilli. Cut into half starting from the tip almost till the end, leaving ½" from the stem end. Cut each half with a scissor into many thin strips, keeping all intact at the base. Put the chilli in chilled water for 4-5 hours in the fridge. It opens up to a flower.

Lemon Twist: *Looks good on a dessert or on a rice dish. Small orange twists too look good.*

Cut a fresh, big and firm lemon into half. Cut a slice from any one piece. Keeping the slice flat on the board, cut halfway from any side of the slice till almost the centre. Holding the slice upright, gently twist the two cut ends in opposite directions to get a twist.

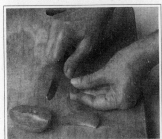

Tomato Butterflies: Cut a firm, longish tomato into 4 long pieces. Holding a piece with pulp side down, from the tip start to cut the skin a little more than halfway. Keep the tomato piece upright with the tip down and the peeled skin away from the pulpy portion, to get a curve on the separated tomato skin.

Coloured Capsicum Baskets: Slice the top of a coloured (yellow, red or green capsicum). Make ½" deep V cuts all around the edge to get a 'VVVV' edge. Leave the bunch of seeds in it as they are. Place on the side of a large platter of salad.

Fruit Bowls for Salads

To make fruit bowls: Make a deep 'V' cut in the centre of the watermelon. To do this, make about 2" slant cut first and then another one a little away from the first one, but which meets at the bottom. Continue cutting in the same way all around the water melon to get a VVVV edge when the two pieces are separated. When cutting, keep the knife tilted and go deep inside. Separate the two pieces. Make the piece hollow, keeping a little red border showing. Cover the empty bowl with a plastic wrap and refrigerate. Fill salad in it at serving time. You may add some chopped watermelon pieces to the salad.

Mango Hedgehogs: Take a ripe, firm mango – avoid using the fibrous variety. Slice off two pieces from either side of the seed. Cut parallel lines with a knife, about ½" apart, along the length of the mango. Cut parallel lines at right angles to these, the same distance apart. You must go right down to the skin, but be extremely careful that you do not cut through the skin. Hold the slice firmly and with the tips of your fingers, push it out from the back, carefully, applying pressure on the thickest part. The slice will open out to resemble a

hedgehog, and will retain this shape. Use this as a garnish to decorate fruit desserts. You can do the same with plums also.

Fruit Fans: Slice a large grape or a strawberry lengthwise into thin slices, cutting almost till the end, but keep the end part of the fruit together. Fan out the slices by pushing the slices gently towards your right, so that they open up like a fan. Place on a dessert or salad.

Fruit Balls: Use a melon scooper to make balls of water melon or mango or papaya and arrange on top of a dessert in a heap.

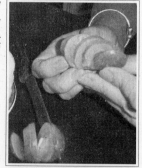

Curry Pastes - Basic Recipes

Although ready-made pastes are now readily available in jars and packets, but they are nothing in taste compared to the home made pastes prepared with fresh ingredients. And ofcourse, they are simple and quick to make in a mixer. You can make these curry pastes well in advance and store them in the fridge for 7-8 days. Use them whenever required.

Red Curry Paste

Gives 1 cup

6-7 dry, red chillies, (preferably the broad Kashmiri variety as it imparts a bright red colour) - break red chillies into two, discard seeds, soak in ¼ cup warm water for 10 minutes
½ onion - chopped, 8-10 flakes garlic - peeled, ½" piece ginger - sliced
1 stick lemon grass - the lower stem is cut into small pieces, discard the leaves or rind of 1 lemon (see page 11), ½ tsp peppercorns (saboot kali mirch)
1 tsp salt, ¼ tsp haldi
1 tbsp coriander seeds (saboot dhania), 1 tsp cumin seeds (jeera), 1 tbsp lemon juice

1. On a tawa, dry roast cumin and coriander seeds on low heat for about 2 minutes till they become aromatic and get roasted but not brown.
2. Put all the other ingredients and roasted seeds in a grinder and churn alongwith the water of the chillies to a smooth paste. Use as required. Store in a glass jar in the fridge.

Green Curry Paste

Gives 1 cup (approx).

6-7 green chillies - deseeded and chopped
½ onion - chopped
1 tbsp chopped garlic, ½" piece ginger - chopped
1 stick lemon grass (use only the lower portion) - cut into pieces, discard the leaves or rind of 1 lemon (see page 11)
2-3 lemon leaves (nimbu ke patte)
½ cup chopped coriander leaves or 1 cup fresh basil leaves
½ tsp salt, 15 peppercorns (saboot kali mirch)
1 tbsp lemon juice, ¼ tsp haldi
1 tbsp coriander seeds (saboot dhania), 1 tsp cumin seeds (jeera)

1. On a tawa, dry roast cumin and coriander seeds on low heat for about 2 minutes till they become aromatic and get roasted but not brown.
2. Put all other ingredients of the curry paste and the roasted seeds in a grinder and grind to a fine paste, using a little water if required.
3. Use as required. Store in a glass jar in the fridge. Can be stored for 1 week.

Yellow Curry Paste

Serves 5- 6

3 tsp turmeric powder (haldi)
1 stick lemon grass (use only the lower portion) - cut into pieces, discard the leaves
or rind of 1 lemon (see page 11)
3 tbsp chopped fresh yellow or red chilli or 6 dried red chillies
½ onion or 2 shallots - finely chopped
8-10 flakes garlic - peeled, 1½" piece ginger or galangal - thinly sliced
1½ tsp coriander seeds (dhania saboot), 1 tbsp lemon juice
1 tsp salt, ¼ tsp peppercorns (saboot kali mirch)
1 star anise (phool chakri) or 1 tsp saunf (fennel seeds)
2 laung (cloves)
1" stick dalchini (cinnamon)
2 tsp five spice powder (see page 13)

1. Put all ingredients of curry paste in a kadhai and dry roast for about 3- 4 minutes.
2. Grind all the roasted ingredients to a paste alongwith 4 tbsp water. Use as required or store in a glass jar in the fridge. Can be stored for 1 week.

Masaman Curry Paste

Serves 4

10 dried, red chillies, rind of 1 lemon (see page 11)
2 medium sized onions - chopped
12-14 flakes of garlic, 4 tsp chopped ginger
2 tbsp cumin seeds (jeera), 2 tsp saunf (fennel seeds)
2" stick dalchini (cinnamon), seeds of 4 moti illaichi (brown cardamom)
4 laung (cloves), 8 saboot kali mirch (black peppercorns)
4 tbsp saboot dhania (coriander seeds)
¼ tsp grated jaiphal (nutmeg)

1. For the paste, roast all ingredients of the paste in a kadhai/wok for 5 minutes or till fragrant. See picture.
2. Grind all the roasted ingredients to a paste alongwith 4 tbsp water. Use as required or store in a glass jar in the fridge. Can be stored for 1 week.

To Prepare Stock:

FRESH VEGETABLE STOCK (MAKES 6 CUPS)

**1 onion - chopped, 1 carrot - chopped, 1 potato - chopped
5 french beans - chopped
½ tsp salt, 7 cups water**

1. Mix all ingredients and pressure cook to give 1 whistle. Reduce heat and cook for 10-15 minutes on low heat. Remove from fire.
2. Do not mash the vegetables if a clear soup is to be prepared. Strain & use as required or store in refrigerator (freezer compartment) for about a week or till further use.

FRESH CHICKEN STOCK (MAKES 5 CUPS)

**bones of 1 chicken, neck and wings
1 bay leaf (tej patta), ½ onion - chopped, ½ tsp salt**

1. Place all the ingredients in a pan with 8 cups of water and bring to a boil. Reduce heat and simmer for 15-20 minutes. Strain and store in a refrigerator till further use. It can also be frozen if you want to keep it for a few days.

READY-MADE STOCK (MAKES 2½ CUPS) ... QUICK STOCK

Vegetarian or chicken soup cubes or seasoning cubes may be boiled with water and used instead of fresh stock, if you are short of time. These seasoning cubes are easily available in the market and are equally good in taste.

**1 seasoning cube (extra taste), chicken or vegetarian (maggi, knorr or any other brand)
2½ cups of water**

1. Crush 1 seasoning cube roughly in a pan.
2. Add 2½ cups of water. Give one boil. Use as required.

Note: The seasoning cube has a lot of salt, so reduce salt if you substitute this stock with the fresh stock. Check taste before adding salt.

Soups

Coconut Fresh Lime

A refreshing Thai drink. Serve it before the soup.

Serves 2

2 cups fresh coconut water
2 tbsp powdered sugar, juice of 1 lemon, ¼ tsp kala namak, 1-2 lemon slices
to coat - some salt and lemon

1. Mix lemon juice, coconut water, sugar and kala namak. Chill in the fridge till serving time.
2. To serve, take a lemon piece and coat the rim of the serving glass with it. Spread salt in a plate and rotate the rim of the glass in the salt.
3. Put lots of ice in a glass. Put 1-2 lemon slices in it. Pour the drink in it. Serve with a straw.

Tip: Do not confuse coconut milk with coconut water. Green coconut is now quite easily available. If fresh coconut is not available, now tetra packs of coconut water are available.

Tom Yum Pla : Recipe on page 27 ➤
Green Mango 'n' Cashew Salad : Recipe on page 30 ➤

Tom Yum

A clear lemon flavoured Thai soup with paper thin slices of vegetables. Prawns can be added for the non vegetarian flavour instead of the vegetables. Cook prawns only for 2-3 minutes, just until they turn pinkish. Even slight overcooking will harden them.

Serves 4   *Picture on opposite page*

3-4 kaffir lemon leaves (nimbu ke patte) - shredded
½ stalk lemon grass - cut into thin slices diagonally, see note below
2-3 mushrooms - cut into paper thin slices
½ small carrot - cut into paper thin diagonal slices
¼ cup of very tiny pieces of broccoli without stem, (cut stem into 1" pieces)
2 fresh red or green chillies - sliced diagonally and deseeded
1 tbsp coriander leaves
2-3 tbsp lemon juice, 2 tsp of sugar
5 cups water, 2 stock cubes
1-2 tsp light soya sauce or fish sauce
¾ tsp salt and ¼ tsp pepper, or to taste
1 tbsp oil, ¼ cup coconut milk (optional)

PASTE (CRUSH TOGETHER)
½ tsp red chilli flakes, 2-3 flakes garlic, ½" piece ginger - finely chopped, ½ tsp salt

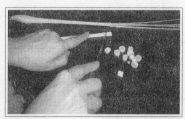

1. Cut mushrooms and carrots into paper thin slices.
2. Prepare a paste by grinding all the ingredients of the paste in a mixer.
3. In a deep pan put 1 tbsp oil, add lemon leaves and lemon grass and the above red chilli paste. Mix well.
4. Add water. Crush stock cubes in it. Give one boil. Reduce heat and keep covered on low heat for 5 minutes.
5. Add mushrooms, carrots, broccoli and fresh red chillies. Boil for 2 minutes on medium flame.
6. Reduce heat. Add lemon juice, light soya sauce, salt, pepper and sugar to taste. Add coriander leaves. Simmer for 1 minute.
7. Add coconut milk. Remove from fire. Pour into individual bowls and serve hot.

Note: *Only the light green stem of lemon grass is edible. The upper grass like portion has a lot of flavour but is not edible. So to use lemon grass, remove the grass portion. Discard 1" hard portion from the base of the stalk of lemon grass and then cut the stalk into thin slices. Tie the remaining grass portion into a knot. You can put this flavourful knot in soups and discard it at serving time.*

◄ ***Tom Yum; Stir Fried Mushrooms with Cashewnuts Salad : Recipe on page 60***

Chicken & Coconut Soup

Picture on page 4   *Serves 4*

3 chicken breasts or 400 gm boneless pieces of chicken
1 onion - finely chopped
2-3 stalks lemon grass - cut into small pieces (see note given below)
3 lemon leaves (nimbu ke patte)
1" piece of ginger - crushed
2 cups ready-made coconut milk
juice of 1 lemon (2 tbsp)
2 tsp brown sugar or 1½ tsp white sugar, 1½ tsp salt, or to taste
1- 2 tsp soya sauce
2 tsp cornflour dissolved in 2 tbsp water

GARNISH
2 fresh red chillies - deseeded and chopped
a few basil leaves (tulsi)

1. Put 7 cups of water, chicken breast or boneless pieces, onion, lemon grass, lemon leaves and ginger in a pressure cooker. Pressure cook to give one whistle. Cook on low heat for 3- 4 minutes. Remove from fire. Let the pressure drop by itself. Open up the cooker and strain the stock into a clean saucepan.

2. Put the stock back on fire, add the coconut milk, stirring until blended. Bring to a boil and then simmer gently over low heat for 10 minutes.

3. Meanwhile, shred the boiled chicken pieces.

4. Add lemon juice, shredded chicken and brown sugar into the soup in the pan.

5. Add soya sauce and dissolved cornflour into the soup. Boil for 2-3 minutes. Serve hot garnished with red chillies and fresh basil leaves.

About Lemon Grass

Only the light green stem of lemon grass is edible. The upper grass like portion has a lot of flavour but is not edible. So to use lemon grass, remove the grass portion. Discard 1" hard portion from the base of the stalk of lemon grass and then cut the stalk into thin slices. Tie the remaining grass portion into a knot. You can put this flavourful knot in soups and discard it at serving time.

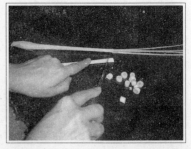

Lemon Coriander Soup

Serves 4

CLEAR STOCK
6 cups water
1 stick lemon grass - chopped or rind of 1 lemon (1 tsp rind)
¼ cup chopped coriander alongwith stalks
1" piece of ginger - washed, sliced without peeling
2 laung (cloves), 1 tej patta (bay leaf)
2 seasoning cubes (maggi or knorr or any other brand)

OTHER INGREDIENTS
1 tbsp oil, ¼ tsp red chilli flakes
½ carrot- - cut into paper thin slices, 2 mushrooms - cut into paper thin slices
2 baby corns - cut into paper thin slices, 1 tsp salt & ¼ tsp pepper, or to taste
2 tbsp lemon juice, 1 tsp sugar, or to taste, 2 tbsp cornflour dissolved in ¼ cup water
2 tbsp coriander leaves - torn roughly with the hands

1. If using lemon rind, wash and grate 1 lemon with the peel gently on the finest side of the grater to get lemon rind. Do not apply pressure and see that the white pith beneath the lemon peel is not grated along with the yellow rind. The white pith is bitter!
2. Cut mushrooms into thin slices.
3. Cut carrot into paper thin slices diagonally (¼ cup).
4. For stock, mix all ingredients given under clear stock with 6 cups of water. Bring to a boil. Keep on low flame for 5 minutes. Strain the stock. If there is lemon grass, pick up most of the pieces and put back in the stock. Keep aside.
5. Heat 1 tsp oil in a wok. Remove from fire. Add ¼ tsp red chilli flakes.
6. Immediately, add carrot, mushrooms and baby corns cut into paper thin slices. Return to fire. Add pepper. Saute for 1 minute on medium flame.
7. Add the prepared stock into the vegetables in the wok. Boil. Add 1 tsp salt and sugar.
8. Add 2 tbsp cornflour dissolved in ¼ cup water, stirring continuously. Boil.
9. Add lemon juice & coriander leaves. Simmer for 1-2 minutes. Check salt, sugar and lemon juice. Add more if required. Remove from fire.
10. Add a few more green coriander leaves. Serve hot in soup bowls.

Prawn Soup

Serves 4-6

300-350 gm uncooked small prawns
4 cups (1 litre) water
3 small lemon leaves (nimbu ke patte)
1 tbsp chopped lemon grass, see note given below
1 tsp fish sauce
2 tbsp fresh lime juice
2 tbsp sliced coriander leaves
1½ tbsp sliced spring onions
½ red chilli - seeded and sliced into 1" strips
salt and pepper to taste

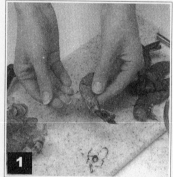

1. Prepare the prawns, shell them and remove the dark vein running along the back. Wash them under running water, drain and pat dry with absorbent kitchen paper. Set aside while you make the soup.
2. Pour the water into a large saucepan and bring to a boil. Add the lime leaves and chopped lemon grass, reduce the heat and simmer for 10 minutes.
3. Add the fish sauce and cook for a further 5 minutes.
4. Add the prawns and lime juice to the pan and cook gently over very low heat for a few minutes, until the prawns become firm and turn a pale pink colour.
5. Add the sliced coriander leaves, spring onions and red chilli strips to the soup.
6. Check the seasonings. Remove from fire. Serve very hot in small bowls.

About Lemon Grass

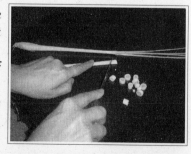

Only the light green stem of lemon grass is edible. The upper grass like portion has a lot of flavour but is not edible. So to use lemon grass, remove the grass portion. Discard 1" hard portion from the base of the stalk of lemon grass and then cut the stalk into thin slices. Tie the remaining grass portion into a knot. You can put this flavourful knot in soups and discard it at serving time.

Tom Yum Pla

Thai hot and sour soup with vegetables and peanuts.

Serves 3-4   *Picture on page 21*

STOCK
1 cup chopped carrot
1 onion - chopped
2 tbsp chopped celery stalks/coriander
1-2 sticks lemon grass - chopped
3-4 lemon leaves (nimbu ke patte)
1½ tsp black peppercorns (saboot kali mirch)

TO BE ADDED TO SOUP
1 medium/3 tbsp carrot - cut into 1" thin pieces
5 large / 100 gms fresh mushrooms - cut into thin, flat slices
3 tbsp bamboo shoots - cut into 1" long, thin pieces - optional
1 tbsp thin slices of ginger
2 tbsp basil leaves
8-10 lemon leaves (nimbu ke patte)
1 tbsp lemon juice
¼ cup roasted peanuts (moongphali) - finely ground to a powder
½ tsp salt or to taste

GRIND TO A PASTE
3 flakes garlic, 2 tbsp chopped coriander leaves
4-5 peppercorns (saboot kali mirch)

1. Put all the ingredients given under stock in a pressure cooker with 6 cups water.
2. Give 3-4 whistles. When the pressure drops, strain the soup without mashing the vegetables, so as to get a clear soup. Keep stock aside.
3. In a pan put 1 tbsp oil and fry the garlic-coriander-peppercorn paste for 1-2 minutes.
4. Add vegetables- carrots, mushrooms, bamboo shoots and ginger. Fry for 1-2 minutes.
5. Add basil and lemon leaves and the prepared stock.
6. Add lemon juice, peanut powder and salt to taste.
7. Let the soup simmer for 15-20 minutes. Serve hot garnished with coriander.

Note: If you like a thicker soup, add 1 tbsp cornflour mixed with ¼ cup water. Boil for 2-3 minutes on low flame after adding cornflour.

Orient Noodle Soup

A spicy, hot, clear soup with lots of vegetables for the winter months. Lemon rind and tomato puree add a delicious flavour to this appetizer soup. Noodles make it different.

Picture on page 4   *Serves 4*

1½ tbsp oil
3 flakes garlic - chopped & crushed
4 mushrooms - sliced and then cut into thin long pieces
1 small carrot - grated, ½ capsicum - finely chopped
10-12 spinach leaves - shredded finely (cut into thin strips)
3 tbsp ready-made tomato puree
½ tsp red chilli flakes
30 gms noodles (½ cup) - break into 2" pieces
1¼ tsp salt, ¼ tsp pepper, 1 tsp sugar
rind of 1 lemon (1 tsp approx.), see step 1
2 tsp green chilli sauce
1 tsp vinegar
2 stock cubes - crushed

1. To take out lemon rind, grate a firm whole lemon on the finest holes of the grater without applying too much pressure. Grate only the upper yellow skin without grating the white bitter pith beneath the yellow skin. Keep rind aside.
2. Heat oil in a pan. Reduce heat and add garlic and red chilli flakes. Saute briefly for ½ minute.
3. Add mushrooms, carrot and capsicum. Stir fry for 1 minute.
4. Add tomato puree and red chillies. Stir for ½ minute.
5. Add 4 cups of water. Crush 2 stock cubes in it. Bring the soup to a boil. Add the noodles. Boil on medium heat for 2-3 minutes till noodles are soft.
6. Add salt, pepper, sugar, lemon rind, chilli sauce and vinegar.
7. Add the finely shredded spinach, simmer for 1 minute. Serve hot in soup bowls.

Tom Yam Gai Soup

Serves 4

2 chicken breasts - make boneless and cut into small pieces
3 tbsp oil
½" piece of ginger - cut into thin strips, 2 tbsp basil leaves (tulsi) - chopped
8-10 lemon leaves (nimbu ke patte), salt to taste
¼ cup roasted peanuts (moongphali) - ground finely
5 cups chicken broth/stock (see page 19)
long slices of red & green chillies for garnishing

PASTE
3 flakes garlic, 4 saboot kali mirch (peppercorns), 1 tsp chopped coriander

1. Grind all ingredients of the paste to a smooth paste in a mixer.
2. Heat 3 tbsp oil. Add the above crushed paste, mix.
3. Add chicken. Stir fry for 3-4 minutes.
4. Add all other ingredients and stock. Simmer for 10-15 minutes.
5. Serve garnished with long slices of red and green chillies.

Note: For a thicker soup, use ½ cup peanuts (moongphali).

Mince Soup

Serves 4

200 gms chicken mince (keema)
4 spring onions - sliced thinly including the greens
7-8 mushrooms - sliced
¼ cup boiled rice
1 tsp pepper (kali mirch), 1 tsp salt, or to taste

STOCK
4 cups water mixed with 2 chicken seasoning cubes (maggi or knorr)

1. Heat 4 tbsp oil in a pan. Add chopped onion including the greens, cook till soft.
2. Add chicken mince and stir fry for 3-4 minutes on high flame. Stir continuously.
3. Add mushrooms and saute for 2 minutes on medium flame.
4. Reduce heat. Add the stock and pepper. Give 1 boil. Check taste and add salt. Simmer for 2 minutes. Keep aside till serving time.
5. At serving time, boil soup. Add boiled rice, bring to a boil. Serve hot.

Green Mango 'n' Cashew Salad

A very unusual and quick salad. Goes well with an Indian meal too. It is generally eaten like a chutney, so make a small bowl for 4-6 people.

Picture on page 21   *Serves 6-8*

3 cups juliennes (match sticks) of raw green, mangoes (3 big mangoes)
½ cup roasted or fried kaju (cashew nuts) or peanuts
1-2 spring onions
OR
½ small onion and ½ capsicum - cut into shreds (thin long strips)
2-3 tbsp mango chutney (you can use home made or ready made)
1-2 dry red chillies - crushed (½ tsp)
1 tsp soya sauce, salt and pepper to taste
3-4 flakes garlic - crushed
1 tsp honey or powdered sugar, if needed

1. Cut white bulb of spring onion into rings and greens into 1" diagonal pieces.
2. Peel green mangoes. Cut the side pieces. Cut into thin match sticks or juliennes. Keep aside.
3. Mix all ingredients except cashew nuts and honey in a bowl. Add sugar or honey if mangoes are very sour. Keep covered in the refrigerator for 2-3 hours for the flavour to penetrate.
4. At serving time, top with roasted or fried nuts and mix lightly.

Note: Ready-made mango chutney is available in the market in small bottles.

Crunchy Salad with Rice Flakes

Serves 4   *Picture on page 2*

½ cup bean sprouts with long shoots (see note given below)
50 gms paneer- cut into ½ "rectangular pieces
¼ cup roasted or fried kaju (cashew nuts)
1- 2 spring onions
½ red and ½ green capsicum - cut into shreds (thin long strips)
½ yellow capsicum - cut into 1" pieces

DRESSING
½ tbsp red chilli flakes, 1 tsp vinegar
1 tbsp soya sauce, ½ tsp salt and ½ tsp pepper or to taste
2 tbsp oil, 2 tbsp honey
1 tsp cumin (jeera), ½ tsp crushed garlic, 2 tbsp water

TOPPING
¼ cup raw rice (kachcha chaawal)

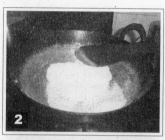

1. To prepare the topping, grind the raw rice to a rough powder in a mixer.
2. Heat a kadhai and put the rice flakes in it. Roast for 4-5 minutes. Keep aside.
3. Cut spring onion into rings till the greens.
4. Deep fry paneer pieces and cashewnuts till golden.

5. Mix all ingredients of the dressing in a small mixer (spice grinder). Churn well to make a paste.
6. Mix all the vegetables, paneer and half of roasted rice in a big bowl. Pour the prepared dressing over it, mix well and chill in the fridge till serving time.
7. At serving time, top with remaining half rice and fried nuts and mix lightly. Serve.

Note: About Bean Sprouts:

Bean Sprouts: These are shoots of moong beans or soya beans. The texture is crisp. To make bean sprouts at home, soak ½ cup of green beans (saboot moong dal) for about 8 hours. Discard water and tie in a muslin cloth. Keep them tied for 2-3 days, remembering to wet the cloth each day. When the shoots are long enough, wash carefully in water. Fresh bean sprouts will keep for several days if refrigerated in a perforated plastic bag.

Glass Noodle Salad

Serves 6-8

3 cups glass noodles or rice vermicelli or thin white bean threads
8-10 french beans - cut into 1" diagonal pieces
100 gm baby corns - sliced diagonally thinly
1 large carrot
1 spring onion - chopped with greens (½ cup)

DRESSING
4 tbsp oil (sesame oil, preferably)
2 tbsp light soya sauce, use just a few drops if using a dark soya sauce
1 tbsp vinegar, 2 tbsp Worcestershire sauce
2 tbsp green chilli sauce, 2 tbsp red chilli sauce
2 tbsp tomato ketchup, 1 tsp crushed garlic
¾ tsp salt, ½ tsp pepper, 1 tsp sugar

TO GARNISH
1 tbsp roasted peanuts (moongphali) - split into two by rolling with a rolling pin (chakla-belan)

1. To boil glass noodles, heat 4 cups of water in a pan with 1 tsp salt. Add noodles to boiling water. Remove from fire. Leave in hot water for 2 minutes or till noodles are slightly soft. Strain and refresh in cold water immediately. Let them be in the strainer for 10 minutes for all the water to drain out.

2. To cut carrot, cut it lengthwise into thin slices. Cut each slice diagonally into 2-3" pieces.

3. Again boil 2 cups water with 1 tsp salt. Add thin, diagonal slices of carrots, baby corns and french beans. When the boil returns after a minute, remove from fire. Strain immediately and refresh by adding cold water. Leave the blanched vegetables in the strainer for 15 minutes for the water to drain out completely.

4. Mix all the ingredients of the dressing. Transfer noodles to a bowl and pour ½ of the dressing over the boiled noodles. Mix well and chill in the fridge for 30 minutes.

5. Add the leftover dressing, blanched vegetables and spring onions to the noodles Mix well and chill till serving time.

6. At serving time, top with some roasted peanuts.

Chicken Noodle Salad

Boil 200 gm of cubed boneless chicken in ½ cup water and ½ tsp salt for 5 minutes or till tender. Strain. Sprinkle 1 tbsp oil and 1 tsp vinegar. Mix well and add to the salad.

Mince Salad

Serves 3-4

200 gms chicken mince (keema)
5 tbsp oil, preferably olive oil
1 onion- cut into round slices and separated into rings
1 tbsp crushed and chopped garlic, 2 spring onions
1 large yellow or green capsicum - cut into 1" square pieces

DRESSING
5-6 basil leaves or ½ tsp dried basil, 1 tbsp soya sauce
1 tsp honey
1 tbsp vinegar (brown), 1 tsp red chilli flakes, ½ tsp salt, ½ tsp pepper

1. Cut bulb of spring onions into circles and the greens into 1" long, diagonal pieces.
2. Heat oil in a pan, add onion rings and garlic. Cook for 1 minute.
3. Add mince. Bhuno for 4-5 minutes on low medium heat till mince gets cooked. Remove from fire.
4. To the onions and mince in the pan, immediately add spring onions along with greens and capsicum. Remove from fire. Mix very well. Arrange in a salad bowl.
5. Mix all the ingredients of the dressing in a small bowl and keep aside.
6. At serving time, pour the dressing over the salad mixture. Mix well and serve cold, at room temperature or warm, according to your liking.

Green Papaya Salad

The popular Thai salad with a chilli-lemon dressing. Choose a hard, raw papaya with a white flesh. Even a slightly ripe papaya with an orangish flesh is not suitable for this salad. Add light soya sauce, so that the salad is not discoloured.

Serves 4-6

3 cups grated hard, raw papaya (1 small kachcha papita), see note given below
1 tomato - cut into 4 pieces and deseeded, cut into small square pieces
½ cup tender green beans (French beans) - sliced very finely
¼ cup roasted peanuts (moongphali)- crushed coarsely

DRESSING
1 tsp fish sauce or light Soya sauce, 3 tbsp lemon juice
4 tbsp sugar syrup, or to taste - (see note)
½ tsp red chilli flakes, ½ tsp salt, or to taste

CRUSH TOGETHER
3-4 red or green chillies and 1 flake garlic

1. Crush together red or green chillies with garlic to a rough paste. Mix this paste with all the other ingredients of the dressing in a flat bowl.
2. Peel and grate papaya from medium holes into thick long shreds. Add chopped beans and tomatoes and papaya to the dressing in the flat dish. Mix well. Cover with a cling film and chill for at least one hour, so that the flavours penetrate.
3. To serve, mix in half the peanuts. Serve topped with rest of the roasted peanuts.

Note: For an authentic papaya salad, peel the papaya and cut into slices. Cut slices into juliennes (matchsticks). To make work simpler, I have grated the papaya. If using dark soya sauce, addd just a few drops to keep the colour light.

Sugar syrup - boil ¼ cup sugar with ¼ cup water. Simmer for 1-2 minutes. Add according to your taste to Thai dishes.

Thai Peanut Corn Cakes

Makes 6-8 corn cakes (kebabs)

¾ cup corn kernels (fresh, tinned or frozen)
¾ cup roasted peanuts (moongphali)
1½ tbsp soya sauce
2 tbsp shredded basil leaves
juice of ½ lemon
1 tbsp ready-made Thai chilli dip (fun food) or ½ tsp sugar
½ tsp red chilli powder, ½ tsp salt, or to taste
4 tbsp cornflour
½ tsp baking powder

1. Grind corn, peanuts, soya sauce, basil, lemon juice, Thai chilli dip or sugar, red chilli powder, salt, cornflour and baking powder in the mixer to a rough paste.

2. Shape into small 1" round kebabs (cutlets). Heat oil in a kadhai and deep fry till golden brown. Serve with hot and sweet dip on page 48.

Veg Satay with Peanut Sauce

Tofu - an important ingredient in Thai cooking is a rich source of proteins for the vegetarians. You can use paneer instead.

Makes 6 Skewers

100 gm tofu or paneer - cubed to get 1½ " squares
6 baby corns, small sized - put in boiling water for 3 minutes and wipe dry
6 mushrooms - trim stalk and keep whole, 1 green capsicum - cut into 1" cubes
6 cherry tomatoes or 1 large, firm tomato cut into 8 pieces and pulp removed

MARINADE
½ tsp salt, ¼-½ tsp red chilli powder, 2 tsp brown sugar or gur
2 fresh red chillies - seeded and thinly sliced
3 tbsp coconut milk
½ tsp soya sauce, 1" piece of ginger - grated
1 tsp lemon juice, 1 tsp brown or ¾ tsp regular sugar, 2 tsp cornflour
8-10 flakes garlic - crushed to a paste
½ tsp jeera powder (ground cumin), ½ tsp dhania powder

PEANUT SAUCE
¼ cup roasted salted peanuts, 1 onion - chopped, ½ tsp salt, ½ tsp red chilli powder
1 tbsp oil, ½-1 tsp sugar, 1 tsp dhania powder, 1 tsp jeera powder (cumin powder)
4-6 flakes garlic - crushed, 1 tbsp butter, 1½ tsp lemon juice, 1 tsp soya sauce
1 cup ready-made coconut milk

1. Boil 3 cups water in a pan, add babycorn and mushrooms in it. Boil for 2-3 minutes. Remove from fire, strain and refresh in cold water.
2. Mix all ingredients of marinade together. Add tofu or paneer, blanched baby corns, mushrooms & tomatoes. Keep covered for ½ hour or till serving time.
3. Thread a mushroom, then a baby corn, then a cherry tomato or regular tomato piece and lastly a paneer piece onto oiled wooden skewers. Leave behind the marinade. Keep aside. Cook in a preheated oven at 180°C/350°F for 6-7 minutes. Baste (pour) with a spoon the remaining marinade on the sticks and cook for another 2-3 minutes.
4. To make peanut sauce, grind peanuts with the salt to a rough powder.
5. Heat 1 tbsp butter in a heavy bottomed small pan or kadhai. Add crushed garlic. Saute till it starts to change colour. Add onion and cook till soft. Reduce heat. Add ½ tsp red chilli powder, dhania powder and jeera powder. Add only ½ cup coconut milk. Boil, stirring. Cook on low heat for 3 minutes, stirring constantly.
6. Add crushed peanuts, ½ tsp sugar, 1½ tsp lemon juice, 1 tsp Soya sauce and remaining ½ cup coconut milk. Boil. Simmer gently for 5 minutes, stirring occasionally to prevent it from sticking to the pan. Serve sauce with satay.

Spring Rolls

Serves 4　　　　　　　　*Picture on page 2*

WRAPPER
1 cup plain flour (maida), ½ cup cornflour
1 tsp salt, 1 tbsp oil, 1 cup water, oil for frying

FILLING
¾ cup seviyaan (vermicelli, Bambino), 1 tbsp soya sauce
¼ cup basil leaves - shredded (use coriander if basil is unavailable)
1 tbsp soya sauce, ½ tsp crushed garlic, ¼ tsp red chilli flakes or powder
½ tsp sugar, ¼ tsp salt to taste, 1 tbsp oil, 2 tbsp crushed peanuts (moongphali)

1. To prepare the wrappers, sift plain flour, cornflour and salt. Add oil and water gradually, mixing to make a dough. Keep aside for ½ hour.

2. Makes small balls from the dough. Roll into thin rotis (rounds). Heat a tawa and put one thinly rolled roti on it. Cook on both sides for 2-3 seconds. Keep rotis covered in a moist cloth in a box.

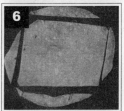

3. To boil seviyaan, boil 4- 5 cups of water. Add 1 tsp salt and 1 tbsp oil and vermicelli. Let it boil for 2 minutes. Remove from fire. Let it be in hot water for 2 minutes. Strain and refresh with cold water. Leave in the strainer for 5 minutes.

4. To make filling, heat 1 tbsp oil and add garlic.

5. Add seviyaan, soya sauce, basils, red chilli powder or flakes, sugar and salt. Mix well. Add crushed peanuts, mix well.

6. To assemble the wrapper, spread a roti on a flat surface. Cut 1" from all the sides to get a square piece.

7. Spread some filling thinly on the upper portion.

8. Fold in ½" from the right and left sides.

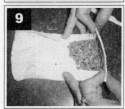

9. Holding on, fold the top part to cover the filling. Roll on to get a rectangular parcel; making sure that all the filling is enclosed.

10. Seal edges with cornflour or maida paste, made by dissolving 1 tsp of cornflour or maida in 1 tsp of water. If you chill the rolls for ½ hour, it keeps better shape.

11. Repeat for the remaining rotis and filling. Cover all with a plastic wrap/cling film and keep aside till serving time.

12. Heat some oil in a large frying pan. Reduce heat and put the rolls, folded side down first in oil. Cook on both sides until crisp and golden. Drain on absorbent paper. Serve with hot and sweet dip on page 48.

Thai Chicken Satay

Chicken on Skewers.

Picture on page 94   *Serves 6*

400 gm chicken - bite sized boneless pieces
6 bamboo skewers - soaked in water to prevent burning

MARINADE
¾ tsp red chilli powder, 2 tsp brown sugar or gur
2 fresh red chillies - seeded and thinly sliced
2 tsp oil
3- 4 tbsp coconut milk powder (maggi) mixed with 2 tbsp milk
1 tsp soya sauce, 1" piece of ginger - grated
1 tbsp lemon juice, 2 tsp cornflour
8-10 flakes garlic - crushed to a paste
1½ tsp jeera powder (ground cumin), 1½ tsp dhania powder

PEANUT SAUCE (SEE PAGE 36)

1. Mix all the marinade ingredients thoroughly in a bowl.
2. Add chicken pieces to the marinade, mix very well. Leave aside for 2 hours in the refrigerator.
3. Thread marinated chicken pieces onto oiled wooden skewers. Do not leave any space between each piece while threading them. Leave behind the marinade.

4. Cook in a preheated grill at 230°C for 10-11 minutes, turning them once in between and basting with the remaining marinade. Alternately, heat a non-stick flat tawa, grease it slightly with a few drops of oil and place skewered chicken, a few at a time. Cook on high heat, turning them frequently. Cook till soft.
5. To make peanut sauce, see page 36 from step 4.

Chicken in Red Thai Curry : Recipe on page 65 ➤

Chicken Spring Rolls

Serves 4

WRAPPER
1 cup plain flour (maida), 1 tsp salt
½ cup cornflour, 1 cup water, 1 tbsp oil, oil for frying

FILLING
½ cup seviyaan (vermicelli) - boiled, ½ cup chicken mince (keema)
½ tsp finely chopped garlic, 1 tsp oyster sauce (optional)
¼ cup basil leaves- shredded, ¼ tsp red chilli flakes or powder
½ tsp salt to taste, ½ tsp sugar, 1½ tbsp soya sauce, 1 tbsp oil
2 tbsp crushed peanuts (moongphali)

1. To prepare the wrappers, sift plain flour, cornflour and salt. Add oil and water gradually, mixing to make a dough. Keep aside for ½ hour.
2. Heat a tawa put one rolled roti on it and cook on both sides for few seconds. Keep the rotis covered in a moist cloth in a box.
3. To boil seviyaan, boil 4-5 cups of water. Add 1 tsp salt, 1 tbsp oil and vermicelli. Let it boil for 2 minutes. Remove from fire. Let it be in hot water for 2 minutes. Strain and refresh with cold water.
4. To make filling, heat 1 tbsp oil. Add garlic.
5. Add chicken mince and cook for 3-4 minutes. Add vermicelli.
6. Add oyster sauce, basil, red chilli flakes, salt, sugar, soya sauce and crushed peanuts. Mix well. Keep aside.
7. To assemble the wrapper, spread a roti on a flat surface. Cut 1" from all the sides to get a square piece.
8. Spread some filling thinly.
9. Fold in ½" from the right and left sides. (See step pictures on page 37).
10. Holding on, fold the top part to cover the filling. Roll on to get a rectangular parcel, making sure that all the filling is enclosed.
11. Seal edges with cornflour or maida paste, made by dissolving 1 tsp of cornflour or maida in 1 tsp of water. If you chill the rolls for ½ hour, it keeps better shape.
12. Repeat for the remaining rotis and filling. Cover all with a plastic wrap/cling film and keep aside till serving time.
13. Heat oil in a large frying pan. Reduce heat and put the rolls, folded side down first in oil. Cook on both sides until crisp and golden. Drain on absorbent paper. Serve with hot and sweet dip given on page 48.

‹ *Green Curry with Chicken and Aubergines : Recipe on page 66*
‹ *Spicy Honey Chicken : Recipe on page 68*

Golden Money Bags

Small balls of dough rolled into small rounds, filled with a filling and given a shape to form a money pouch. Starter with an impressive look.

Gives 15 pouches

POUCHES
1 cup maida (plain flour)
½ cup suji (semolina)
a pinch of soda-bi-carb (mitha soda)
½ tsp salt
1 tbsp oil & oil for frying

FILLING
1 tsp crushed garlic
2 tbsp carrots - grated
2 boiled potatoes - mashed roughly
1 tsp soya sauce
½ tsp salt, ¼ tsp pepper, ½ tsp sugar
2 tbsp roasted peanuts (moongphali)- pounded/crushed
1 tbsp chopped coriander

1. Heat 1 tbsp oil. Reduce heat and add the crushed garlic. Stir for a few seconds.
2. Add carrots and mix.
3. Add potatoes, Soya sauce, salt, pepper and sugar. Cook for 2-3 minutes. Add peanuts and coriander. Cool, adjust seasonings to taste & keep aside.
4. Mix all ingredients of the pouches and make a dough with warm water (like chappati dough). Keep aside covered for 30 minutes.
5. Make around 15 small balls and roll one at a time into a small round.
6. Put a teaspoon of filling in the centre and pick up the sides and press at the neck to form a money pouch. Tie the neck with a thin blade of lemon grass if you have.
7. Deep fry to a golden brown colour.
8. Serve hot with a spicy tomato sauce (you may mix 2 tbsp tomato ketchup with 1 tsp red chilli sauce).

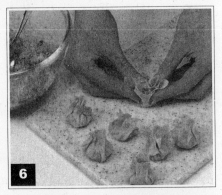

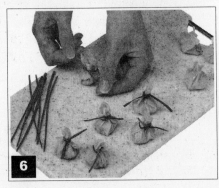

Crispy Soft Corn

Serves 4

FILLING
2 cups ready-made cream style sweet corn (1 tin, see note)
½ tsp garlic paste (3-4 flakes of garlic- crushed)
¼ tsp salt, ¼ tsp pepper, or to taste
2 tbsp cornflour mixed with 4- 5 tbsp water
BATTER
½ cup maida or cornflour
¼ tsp haldi, a pinch of salt, ½ cup cold water

1. Heat 2 tbsp oil in a pan, add garlic paste and stir on medium flame.
2. Add cream style sweet corn, mix.
3. Add salt and pepper. Mix well and cook for 2-3 minutes on medium flame.
4. Add cornflour paste. Cook for 2 minutes. Remove from fire. Check salt. Let it cool.
5. Put the cooled mixture in a small mixer and grind to a smooth paste.
6. Spread the mixture in a flat plate. Keep in the fridge for atleast 2-3 hours to set.
7. Mix all ingredients of the batter in a bowl.
8. Cut the set mixture carefully into 2" square pieces, (approx. 8-10 pieces). Dip each piece in maida batter and deep fry each piece immediately in hot oil till golden.

Note: The leftover corn, can be stored in an air tight box in the freezer compartment of the fridge for about 2 months or till further use.

Toasted Chilli Cashews

Serves 6

125 gms cashewnuts (kaju)
¼ tsp finely chopped garlic
1 dry red chilli - crushed
2 small fresh green chillies - remove seeds and chop finely
1 spring onion - finely chopped uptill the greens, (keep greens separate)
salt to taste

1. Heat a kadhai on fire. Add cashews and roast till it just starts to change colour. Remove from fire.
2. In another wok/kadhai, heat 1 tbsp oil, reduce heat. Add garlic, white of spring onion, dry red chilli, and green chillies, fry till garlic turns golden brown.
3. Add the roasted cashews and the spring onion greens. Mix well.
4. Add salt to taste. Remove from fire. Serve warm.

Batter Fried Prawns

Serves 4

(250 gms) 12 large prawns - cleaned & deveined

MARINADE
1 tbsp soya sauce, 1 tbsp wine or sherry
¼ tsp ajinomoto (optional), ½ tsp salt, ¼ tsp black pepper

BATTER
1 egg
3 tbsp plain flour *(maida)*
3 tbsp cornflour
1 tbsp oil, ¼ tsp white pepper, ¼ tsp salt
¼ tsp ajinomoto (optional)
1 tbsp sesame seeds *(til)*

1. In a bowl mix soya sauce, sherry, ajinomoto, salt and black pepper. Marinate the prawns in it for 15-30 minutes.
2. Make a smooth paste by mixing all the ingredients of the batter - egg, flour, cornflour, oil, white pepper, salt, ajinomoto and sesame seeds Add just enough water to get a very thick batter such that it is of a coating consistency.
3. Dip the prawns into the batter.
4. Deep fry 4-5 pieces at a time for about 2 minutes, till golden brown & immediately remove from oil. Serve hot with chilli sauce.

Note: If desired you can let the tail remain and then marinate the prawns.

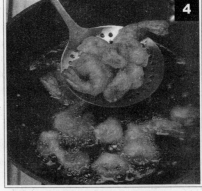

Vegetable Dim Sums

A steamed snack. Use a steamer basket or an idli stand for steaming them.

Makes 14 pieces

DOUGH
1 cup maida, 1 tbsp oil, ¼ tsp salt

FILLING
2 tbsp oil
1 onion - finely chopped
4-5 mushrooms - finely chopped, optional
1 large carrot - grated
2 green chillies - finely chopped
1 tsp ginger-garlic paste
2 cups grated cabbage (½ small cabbage)
1 tsp salt & ½ tsp pepper powder, or to taste
1 tsp lemon juice

DIPPING SAUCE
4-5 tbsp Soya sauce, 2 tbsp white vinegar, 1-2 tbsp oil
4 flakes garlic - crushed to a paste, ½ tsp chilli powder, ¼ tsp salt
2 tsp tomato ketchup

1. For the dough, sift maida with salt. Add oil and knead with enough water to make a stiff dough of rolling consistency, as that for puris.
2. For the filling, heat oil. Add chopped onion. Fry till soft. Add mushrooms and cook further for 2 minutes. Add carrot, green chillies & ginger-garlic paste. Mix well and add the cabbage. Stir fry on high flame for 3 minutes. Add salt, pepper to taste. Add lemon juice and mix well. Remove from fire and keep filling aside.
3. Take out the dough and form small balls. Roll out flat, as thin as possible into small rounds of 2½" diameter.
4. Put some stuffing in the centre and make it into a ball. Roll the ball between the hands to give it an elongated shape like a roll.
5. To steam, put them in idlis stands or a steamer & steam for 10 minutes.
6. Cool the dimsums. Cut a slice from the top to expose the filling. Dot with chilli sauce.
7. For dipping sauce, mix all ingredients in a bowl. Serve with dimsums.

FINAL RECIPE

Fish Cakes with Cucumber Relish

A great favourite of my family. These wonderful small fish cakes are a familiar and a very popular appetizer of Thailand.

Makes 12-14 cakes (patties)

300 gm boneless fish - cut into small pieces
1 star anise (phool chakri) or ½ tsp saunf, 1" stick cinnamon (dalchini)
2-3 lemon leaves (nimbu ke patte)
5 tbsp red curry paste (see page 17) or 2 tsp red chilli paste (use 4-5 dry red chillies for it)
1 egg
50 gms beans (French beans) - chopped finely
6 tbsp cornflour
2 tbsp fish sauce or 1 tbsp soya sauce
2-3 big flakes of garlic - chopped
1 tsp salt, ½ tsp sugar/gur
3 lemon leaves (nimbu ke patte) - shredded or cut into very small pieces (optional)
2 tbsp coriander leaves chopped

CUCUMBER RELISH (GIVES 1¼ CUPS)
4 tbsp vinegar, 4 tbsp water, 2 tbsp sugar, 1 tsp salt
2-3 flakes garlic - paste or minced
1 small cucumber (kheera) - cut into thin slices or very small pieces
4 shallots/1 small onion - finely sliced or chopped
½ tbsp finely chopped ginger, 2 green/red chillies - sliced

1. Heat a pan of water with anise, cinnamon and lemon leaves.
2. When it boils, add fish. Let it cook for 4-5 minutes. Remove fish from water, when skin can be removed easily. Remove skin. (If using skinless fish it can be used raw).
3. Put fish, curry paste and egg in the mixer and churn well to get a smooth mixture. Transfer to a bowl. Mix all other ingredients including beans & cornflour. Mix

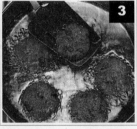

   well. Shape into small patties & deep fry till golden brown.
4. To prepare the relish, cook together vinegar, water, sugar and salt. When sugar dissolves, give 2-3 boils and remove from heat. Cool.
5. Add all the other ingredients and mix well.
6. Serve hot fish cakes with cucumber relish or any dip of your choice.

Note: If patties break on frying, increase the cornflour by 1-2 tbsp.

Golden Mince Pouches

These crisp delicious pouches are served as an appetizer or as an accompaniment with drinks.

Gives 15 pouches

POUCHES
1 cup maida (flour)
½ cup suji (semolina)
a pinch of soda-bi-carb (mitha soda)
½ tsp salt, 1 tbsp oil

FILLING
1 tbsp butter/oil
225 gms mince (mutton or chicken or pork)
1 tbsp chopped garlic
½ tsp salt or adjust to taste
1 tsp red chilli paste or chill powder
2 tbsp chopped spring onion/onion
1 tbsp fish sauce or 1 tsp soya sauce
1 tsp sugar/gur
8-10 long chives - chopped (optional)
some freshly ground pepper (optional)
1 tbsp chopped fresh coriander

1. Mix all ingredients of the pouches and make a dough with water (like chapati dough). Keep aside covered.
2. Heat oil in a cooker. Add garlic. Fry for 1-2 minutes.
3. Add mince, salt, red chilli paste and 3-4 tbsp water.
4. Give 3-4 whistles. Cool and open the cooker. Add all the other ingredients, seasonings and cook till it dries completely.
5. Cool, adjust seasonings to taste and keep aside.
6. Make small balls around 15 and roll one at a time into a small rounds.
7. Put filling in the centre and pick up the sides and press at the neck to form a money pouch. Tie the neck with a thin lemon grass.
8. Deep fry 5-6 pieces at a time on medium flame to a golden brown colour.
9. Serve hot with sauce or any of the dips of your choice.

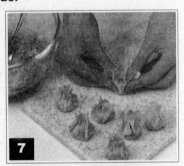

Hot and Sweet Dip

A traditional Thai dip flavoured with crushed red chilli and sugar.

Makes 1½ cups

2 tbsp vinegar, ¾ cup sugar
1 cup water, 1 tbsp red chilli flakes, 1 tbsp salt

1. Combine the vinegar, sugar and water and boil till the mixture becomes a thick syrup.
2. Cool slightly, add the crushed red chillies and the salt.
3. Allow to stand for atleast 6 hours before using. Adjust the vinegar and chillies to your taste.

Sweet and Sour Dip

Combine this sweet and tangy dip with any deep-fried Thai starter.

Makes ½ cup (approx.)

a lemon sized ball of imli (tamarind)
½ cup gur, ½ tsp lemon juice
½ tsp salt, ¼ tsp red chilli powder

1. Boil ¼ cup water and imli in a pan. Give one boil. Remove from fire.
2. Strain through a sieve (channi), mashing with the back of a spoon to get pulp.
3. In another pan put 1 tbsp of imli pulp, gur, salt, red chilli powder and ¼ cup water. Give one boil. Remove from fire. Add lemon juice. Chill and serve.

Peanut Dip

A spicy sweet peanut dip flavoured with lemon grass and coconut.

Makes 1 cup

¼ cup roasted salted peanuts
½ tsp salt, ¾ tsp red chilli powder
1 tsp dhania powder, 1 tsp jeera (cumin)
1 tbsp butter, 4-6 flakes garlic - crushed
1 onion - chopped, ¾ cup milk, ½ tsp sugar, 1 tsp lemon juice, ½ tsp soya sauce

1. Grind peanuts, salt, chilli powder, dhania powder & jeera in a mixer.
2. Heat butter in a kadhai. Add crushed garlic. Add onion, cook till it turns soft. Add peanut paste, mix.
3. Add milk, cook stirring on low heat for 3-4 minutes, stirring constantly.
4. Add sugar, lemon juice and Soya sauce, stirring. Remove from fire. Serve at room temperature.

Vegetable Curries

Thai Red Curry

Picture on cover   *Serves 4-6*

RED CURRY PASTE

**4 Kashmiri red chillies - deseeded & soaked in ½ cup warm water for 10 minutes
½ onion - chopped, 8-10 flakes garlic - peeled, ½" piece ginger - sliced
1 stalk lemon grass or rind of 1 lemon (see page 11)
1½ tsp coriander seeds (dhania saboot), 1 tsp cumin (jeera)
1 tbsp lemon juice, 6 peppercorns (saboot kali mirch), 1 tsp salt**

VEGETABLES

**100 gms paneer or tofu - cut into 1" square pieces and deep fried till golden brown
6-8 baby corns - slit lengthwise, 1 carrot - diagonally sliced
1 small broccoli or ½ cauliflower - cut into small florets (about 8 pieces)
5-6 mushrooms - sliced or 8- 10 French beans - cut into 1" pieces
¼ cup chopped bamboo shoots (optional)**

OTHER INGREDIENTS

**2½ cups thin coconut milk (use readymade coconut milk or for fresh see step 2)
½ tsp soya sauce, 15 basil leaves, 5-6 lemon leaves (nimbu ke patte)
1 tbsp oil, salt to taste, 1 tsp brown sugar or ½ tsp regular sugar, or to taste**

1. Dry roast coriander and cumin seeds on a tawa till they turn light golden and fragrant. Add all the other ingredients of the red curry paste and grind along with the water in which the chillies were soaked, to a very fine paste.
2. Extract coconut milk by soaking 1 grated coconut in 2 cups of warm water. Blend and then strain through a muslin cloth. To the left over coconut and 1 more cup of warm water. Repeat to get 2½-3 cups of milk. You can use readymade coconut milk also.
3. Heat the oil in a large pan, add the red curry paste and stir fry for 2-3 minutes on low heat.
4. Add 2 tbsp of coconut milk. Add vegetables and cook for 2-3 minutes.
5. Add the rest of the coconut milk, soya sauce and lemon leaves.
6. Simmer on low heat for 5-7 minutes till the vegetables are tender.
7. Add fried paneer or tofu, salt and sugar to taste. Add basil leaves. Boil for 1-2 minutes. Serve hot garnished with red chilli slices with steamed rice or noodles.

Note: You can use any vegetables of your choice.

The red curry paste can be made extra and store in an airtight container (for upto 1 month). Alternatively, freeze for upto 3 months. To obtain a bright red curry paste, use red Kashmiri chillies as for as possible. A little orange red colour may be added if you do not get a bright red curry.

Thai Green Curry

Serves 4

100 gms tofu or paneer - cut into 1" fingers
½ zucchini - sliced diagonally
½ small cauliflower - cut into small florets
6 baby corns - halved lengthwise, 1 carrot - diagonally sliced
8-10 French beans - very diagonaly cut into 1" pieces
2½ cups ready-made coconut milk or use ½ cup water with 2 cups coconut milk if milk is too creamy
1 tbsp finely chopped lemon grass
1 tsp salt, 3 tsp sugar or gur
½ -1 tsp soya sauce
3 tbsp chopped fresh basil
2-3 green or red chillies - slit long for garnishing

GREEN CURRY PASTE
5-6 green chillies - chopped, ½ onion - chopped
1 tbsp chopped garlic, ½" piece ginger - chopped
1 stick lemon grass (use only the lower portion) - cut into pieces, discard the leaves
½ tsp salt, ¼ tsp haldi
15 peppercorns (saboot kali mirch), 1 tbsp lemon juice
1 tbsp coriander seeds (saboot dhania), 1 tsp cumin seeds (jeera)
2-3 lemon leaves (nimbu ke patte) or 1 tsp lemon rind
1 cup fresh basil leaves or ½ cup chopped coriander leaves

1. For the green curry paste, dry roast coriander and cumin seeds for 2 minutes on a tawa till fragrant but not brown. Put all other ingredients of the curry paste and the roasted seeds in a grinder and grind to a fine paste, using a little water.
2. Heat 3 tbsp oil in a kadhai. Add green curry paste. Fry for 2-3 minutes.
3. Add cauliflower. Fry for 3-4 minutes. Add other vegetables and stir for 1 minute. Add 1 cup coconut milk. Stir on low heat for 2-3 minutes.
4. Add chopped lemon grass, salt, sugar and the rest of coconut milk. Boil. Add soya sauce. Cook on low heat for a few minutes or till vegetables are crisp tender.
5. Add basil, tofu or paneer. Give 2-3 boils.
6. Garnish with sliced red or green chillies (long thin slices), basil leaves.
7. Serve hot with boiled/steamed rice.

Note: Discard 1" from the bottom of the lemon grass. Peel a few outer leaves. Chop into small pieces uptil the stem. Discard the upper grass like portion.

Masaman Curry

Serves 6

6-7 tbsp masaman curry paste (see page 18)
150 gms babycorn - cut into 1" pieces
250 gms broccoli - cut into medium sized florets (1" pieces)
4 tbsp oil
1 cup thick coconut milk or coconut cream
3½ cups ready-made coconut milk
1 tbsp chopped lemon grass or rind of 1 lemon (see page 11)
1-2 tsp sugar/gur (adjust to taste)
5 tbsp tamarind juice (imli juice)
2 black cardamoms (moti illaichi)
1½" cinnamon stick (dalchini)
1 large onion - cut into 8 pieces & each piece separated to get onion leaves
1½ tsp salt, or to taste
½ tsp haldi powder (optional) - gives a better colour if used
50 gms (½ cup) roasted peanuts (moongphali) - roughly crushed

1. Heat 4 tbsp oil in a kadhai, add masaman curry paste and ½ tsp haldi. Fry for 2 minutes.
2. Add babycorn and broccoli pieces and stir fry for 2-3 minutes.
3. Add coconut milk, chopped lemon grass and upper grass like portion tied into a knot.
4. Except roasted peanuts add all the other ingredients & cook on low heat for 3-4 minutes.
5. Add roasted peanuts. Cook for 2 minutes and serve hot with rice.

Vegetable Yellow Curry

Serves 5

½ recipe of yellow curry paste (see page 18)
4 tbsp oil
1" piece of ginger - peeled & sliced thinly
2 tbsp roasted peanuts (moongphali) - roughly crushed
1 vegetable seasoning cube (maggi or knorr) - crushed to a powder
1½ cups ready-made coconut milk
1 cup water
5-6 lemon leaves (nimbu ke patte)
1 tbsp finely chopped lemon grass (use only stem, see note given on page 51)
15 basil leaves - chopped or coriander leaves
1 tsp brown sugar or regular sugar

VEGETABLES

1 tiny flower of cauliflower or broccoli (200 gms) - cut into small florets
100 gms babycorn - each cut into 2 pieces, lengthwise
¼ cup tinned bamboo shoots (optional)

1. Heat 4 tbsp oil in a kadhai. Add yellow curry paste. Fry for 3-4 minutes on low heat.
2. Add ginger, peanuts, seasoning cube and vegetables. Mix well for 2 minutes.
3. Add coconut milk, water, lemon leaves, chopped lemon grass, basil leaves and sugar. Give 3- 4 boils. Serve hot garnished with a red chilli flower or slices with steamed rice or noodles.

Cashew Chill Curry

Serves 4

2 potatoes, ½ cup soya nuggets - soak in hot water for ½ hour
½ tsp haldi powder (turmeric powder)
1 cup coconut milk, 1 cup water
1 tbsp finely chopped lemon grass (use only stem, see page 51)
4 tbsp cashews (kaju)- ground to a smooth paste in a mixer with 5 tbsp water
½ recipe of masaman curry paste (see page 18)
1¼ tsp sugar/gur (adjust to taste)
1¼ tsp salt, or to taste

BATTER
¼ cup maida, ¼ cup cornflour
½ tsp salt, ¼ tsp pepper, ½ tsp soya sauce
¼ tsp haldi

1. Peel the potatoes and cut into ¼" thick slices. Cut each slice into ¼" wide fingers. Soak them in salted cold water for 15 minutes. Strain and wipe dry on a clean kitchen towel. Sprinkle 1-2 tbsp cornflour on them to absorb excess water.

2. For batter- mix flour, cornflour, salt, pepper, ajinomoto, soya sauce and haldi. Add just enough water, about 3-4 tbsp, to make a batter of a thick pouring consistency, such that it coats the potatoes.

3. Dip fingers of potatoes in the batter and deep fry to a golden colour. Check that they get properly cooked on frying. Keep aside, spread out on a plate till the time of serving.

4. To the same kadhai add 3 tbsp oil, masaman curry paste, soya nuggets and haldi. Fry for 2-3 minutes till aromatic and leaves oil.

5. Add cashew paste. Mix well.

6. Add coconut milk, water, chopped lemon grass and grassy upper portion of the same lemon grass tied into a knot. Give 2 boils.

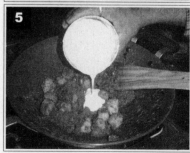

7. Add all other ingredients and cook on low heat for 2 minutes. Remove from fire.

8. At serving time add potatoes to hot curry. Serve.

Bean Curd & Pineapple in Northern Style Curry

Serves 4

250 gms bean curd (tofu) or paneer
½ of a small pineapple - cut into 1" pieces (1 cup)
100 gms bamboo shoots (use tin) - cut into thin slices, optional
3 tbsp oil
¾" piece of ginger - cut into paper thin slices (use only 4-5 slices)
1 lemon sized ball of imli (tamarind) soaked in 1 cup water
1½ cups coconut milk
1½ cups water

PASTE
3 tsp chopped garlic, 3 onions
2 tsp salt, 3 dry red chillies
2 tbsp finely chopped lemon grass, 2 tsp curry powder
1 tbsp soya sauce
1 tbsp brown sugar or regular sugar

1. Grind all the ingredients written under paste to a smooth paste. Use a little water if required.
2. Cut the bean curd (tofu) or paneer into 1" square pieces.
3. Peel the pineapple, remove the eyes and core. Cut into 2" pieces.
4. Boil 1 cup water and add a ball of imli, give 2-3 boils. Strain well through a sieve (channi). Keep strained water aside.
5. Heat oil in wok/kadhai, add sliced ginger, fry for 2- 3 minutes.
6. Add prepared paste, cook for 10 minutes.
7. Add imli juice, cook for 2- 3 minutes.
8. Add 1½ cups coconut milk and pineapple, give 2 boils.
9. Add 1½ cups water. Boil.
10. Add paneer, mix. Serve hot.

Vegetables in Thick Masala Curry

Serves 4

200 gms mushrooms - cut each into two pieces
200 gms capsicum - cut into ½" slices
1 fresh nariyal (coconut) - grated
4 shredded kaffir lemon leaves (nimbu ke patte)
4 tbsp oil
upper grass portion of 1 lemon grass - tied into a knot (use the edible lower part in the paste)

CURRY PASTE
1 tbsp soya sauce
1 tbsp grated gur or brown sugar or ½ tbsp regular sugar
4 lemon leaves (nimbu ke patte)
5 large dry red chillies
5 onions
10 flakes garlic, 1 tsp chopped ginger
2 tbsp chopped lemon grass (see page 11)
1 tsp lemon rind (see page 11)
2 tsp finely chopped coriander
6 peppercorns (saboot kali mirch), 1 tsp salt

1. Grind all ingredients written under curry paste to a smooth paste in a mixer.
2. Grind grated coconut with 2 cups of water in a mixer. Strain the coconut paste through a muslin cloth. Keep coconut milk aside.
3. Cut each mushroom into half.
4. Heat 4 tbsp oil in a wok/kadhai, add the curry paste and fry for 5-6 minutes.
5. Add the mushrooms & cook for 2-3 minutes.
6. Add prepared coconut milk, capsicum, lemon leaves and 1 cup water.
7. Add knotted lemon grass. Give 2 boils. Check salt. Remove from fire. Remove tied lemon grass. Serve hot.

Chicken Stirred with Cashewnuts : Recipe on page 72 ➤

Lotus Stem in Panang Curry

Serves 4

200 gm lotus stem (Bhein) - buy those which are closed at both ends
2 cups milk
1 tbsp finely chopped lemon grass (use only stem, see page 11)
½ cup cream, ½ cup water

BATTER
4 tbsp cornflour
4 tbsp plain flour (maida)
½ tsp salt, ¼ tsp pepper
2 flakes garlic - crushed to a paste
¼ cup water

PANANG CURRY PASTE
1 tsp jeera (cumin seeds), ½ tsp coriander seeds
4 onions - chopped, 8 flakes garlic - chopped
10 dry, red chillies - deseeded
1 lemon grass - chopped (see page 11)
3 tbsp chopped coriander, 1" piece of ginger - chopped
2 tbsp roasted peanuts, 2 tbsp oil, 2 tsp saunf or 1 star anise (phool chakri)

1. For the paste, dry roast cumin and coriander seeds on low heat on a tawa till they become aromatic and get roasted but not brown, for about 2 minutes.
2. Put all other ingredients of the curry paste and the roasted seeds in a grinder and grind to a fine paste, using a little water if required.
3. Peel lotus stem and cut diagonally into paper thin slices. Wash well.
4. Mix all ingredients of the batter together.
5. Wipe dry the vegetable with a clean kitchen towel. Dip each piece in batter. Deep fry in two batches to a golden yellow colour. Do not brown them. Keep aside.

6. Heat oil in a kadhai, add panang paste, cook for 4-5 minutes.
7. Add milk, chopped lemon grass, cream and water. Give 2-3 boils. Keep aside till serving time.
8. To serve, add cream to the curry and bring to a boil on low heat. Add lotus stem to hot curry, mix. Check salt. Remove from fire. Serve hot.

Note: Panang paste can be stored for 1 week in the fridge.

◁ Prawns in Garlic Sauce : Recipe on page 80

Stir Fried Mushrooms with Cashewnuts

A dry preparation of mushrooms. Ideal as a side dish. The cashewnuts add a lot of crunch to the dish.

Picture on page 22   *Serves 4*

200 gms mushrooms - each cut into 2 pieces
¼-½ cup freshly roasted or fried kaju (cashewnuts)
1 large green or ½ green and ½ red capsicum - cut into ¾" squares
2 spring onions - cut bulb into 4 pieces and greens into 1" long pieces
3 tbsp oil
1 tbsp chopped & lightly crushed garlic
1 tbsp finely chopped ginger
½ tsp salt & ¼ tsp peppercorns - crushed
½ tsp sugar
1 tbsp vinegar, 1 tsp Soya sauce
4 fresh red chillies - slit lengthwise, optional

1. Heat 3 tbsp oil in a pan or kadhai. Add white part of onion till onion turns light brown. Add garlic and ginger. Stir.
2. Add mushrooms, ½ tsp salt and ¼ tsp pepper. Stir fry on high flame, keeping them spaced apart, for 4-5 minutes till light brown and the water evaporates, and they turn dry.
3. Reduce heat. Add sugar, vinegar and Soya sauce.
4. Add green and red capsicums, cashewnuts, greens of spring onion and red chillies.
5. Sprinkle ¼ tsp of salt. Saute for 1-2 minutes. Serve hot.

Crispy Vegetables

Serves 6

Picture on page 1

½ of a cauliflower or broccoli - cut into 1" florets
4 large mushrooms - cut each piece into 2 from the middle
8 babycorns - keep whole
½ red, ½ yellow capsicum, ½ green capsicum - cut into 1" square pieces
1 onion - cut into 8 pieces
20 basil leaves - keep whole, remove stem, 1 tsp garlic paste

BATTER

¼ cup rice flour or ¼ cup raw rice (kachcha chaawal) - ground to a powder in a mixer
1 tbsp chopped lemon grass
¾ cup cornflour, 1 tsp soya sauce
¾ cup chilled water- approx., 1 tbsp oil
½ tsp red chilli flakes, ¾ tsp salt

PASTE

1 tbsp lemon juice, 1 tbsp oil
4 dry, red chillies, 1 tbsp black bean sauce
3 tbsp ready-made mango chutney
1 tsp soya sauce
1" stick cinnamon (dalchini)
1 tbsp tomato ketchup, 1 tsp honey
½ tsp salt

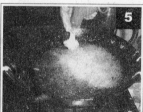

1. Cut all vegetables as written above.
2. Put all ingredients written under paste in a mixer and grind to a paste.
3. Use ready-made riceflour or roughly grind ½ cup rice in a mixer to a powder. Roast this ground rice in a kadhai till it starts to change colour. Sieve the roasted rice to get a fine powder.

4. Mix all ingredients of batter in a bowl. Mix well and add cauliflower, baby corns and mushrooms to the batter and keep aside for 30 minutes or more.
5. Heat oil in a kadhai. Mix the vegetables in the batter well and deep fry till golden brown.
6. At serving time, heat 1 tbsp oil. Add 1 tsp garlic paste & onions. Stir fry for 2 minutes. Add the capsicums. Stir.

7. Add the mango chutney paste. Stir fry for 2 minutes.
8. Add ¼ cup water.
9. Add fried vegetables and basil, mix well and serve hot.

Orange Glazed Sesame Vegetables

Stir-fried vegetables in a tangy orange sauce with peanuts and sesame seeds.

Serves 4

½ cup paneer - cut into thin long strips
1 cup broccoli (hari gobhi) or cauliflower - cut into small florets
6 babycorns - sliced diagonally
1 green capsicum - cut into 1" square pieces
1 cup mushrooms - sliced
1 tbsp finely chopped lemon grass (use only stem, see page 11)
2 tbsp soya sauce
1 cup ready-made orange juice (tropicana or real)
1 tsp cornflour
2 tbsp roasted sesame seeds (white til)
2 tbsp peanuts (moongphali)
¾ tsp salt and ½ tsp pepper or to taste
a pinch of sugar to taste

1. Roast sesame seeds and peanuts on a hot tawa till golden. Remove from fire and keep aside.
2. Heat 3 tbsp oil in a large pan or wok, add the paneer strips and stir fry till they turn brown. Remove paneer from pan, keep aside.
3. To the same pan, add the broccoli, babycorn, capsicum, mushrooms and lemon grass. Stir fry for 1 to 2 minutes.

4. Mix soya sauce, orange juice and cornflour in a cup. Stir this mixture into the vegetables. Cook stirring for 4-5 minutes till the sauce has thickened and glaze develops.

Cutting of all vegetables

5. Add sesame seeds, peanuts, salt, pepper and sugar to taste. Add paneer. Cook for 2 minutes. Serve hot with rice or noodles.

Golden Fried Tofu in Bean Sauce

Serves 4

200 tofu or paneer - cut into 1" square pieces
3 onions - chopped finely
3 flakes garlic - finely chopped
1 tsp grated ginger
1 fresh red or green chilli - remove seeds and finely chopped
2 tbsp chopped lemon grass stems (see page 11)
100 gm flat beans or regular beans - cut into 1" pieces
1 tbsp soya sauce, 1 tbsp tomato ketchup, 4 tbsp black bean sauce
¼ tsp each of salt & pepper or to taste

1. Deep fry tofu or paneer till golden brown.
2. Heat 3 tbsp oil in a kadhai or wok, add onions, garlic, ginger, chilli and lemon grass for 2-3 minutes.
3. Add the beans, stir well and fry for 2-3 minutes.
4. Add the soya sauce, tomato ketchup, black bean sauce, and 6 tbsp water. Add salt & pepper Mix well.
5. At serving time, add fried paneer, mix and serve hot.

Tip: For the best flavour, soak the lemon grass stalks in a little warm water for 30 minutes before using.

Red Vegetables

Serves 4

6 tbsp red curry paste or masaman curry paste (see page 17 or 18)
2 onions - each cut into 8 pieces
4 toris/zuchhini/courgettes (200 gm) -peeled and sliced
1 tbsp finely chopped lemon grass (use only stem, see page 11)
3 carrots - sliced
15 beans - each cut into 1" long pieces
1½ tbsp soya sauce, 1 tsp honey, 1 tsp vinegar
¼ tsp pepper, ½ tsp salt or to taste

1. Heat 6 tbsp oil in a pan, add onion and stir till golden.
2. Add red or masaman curry paste, fry for 3-4 minutes.
3. Add tori, lemon grass, carrots and beans. Cook for 3-4 minutes.

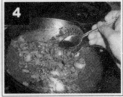

4. Add soya sauce, honey, vinegar, ¼ tsp pepper, ½ tsp salt and ½ cup water. Cook for 3-4 minutes. Remove from fire.

Chicken Curries 'n' Stir Fries

Chicken in Red Thai Curry

Serves 4-6   *Picture on page 39*

400 gms boneless chicken- cut into ¾" small pieces
½ of a small broccoli or cauliflower - cut into florets (about 6 pieces)
5-6 mushrooms - sliced or 8-10 French beans - cut into 1" pieces
¼ cup chopped bamboo shoots (optional)

RED CURRY PASTE
8 Kashmiri red chillies - deseeded & soaked in ¾ cup warm water for 10 minutes
1 onion - chopped, 15-16 flakes garlic - peeled, 2" piece ginger - sliced
2 stalk lemon grass or rind of 2 lemon (see page 11)
3 tbsp coriander seeds (dhania saboot), 2 tbsp vinegar
2 tsp cumin (jeera), 12 peppercorns (saboot kali mirch), 2 tsp salt

OTHER INGREDIENTS
5½ cups ready-made coconut milk mixed with 2 tbsp cornflour
2-4 tbsp fish sauce (optional)
1 tsp soya sauce, 20-25 basil leaves - chopped or coriander leaves
8-9 lemon leaves, 2 tbsp oil, salt to taste, 1¾ tsp brown sugar or 1 tsp regular sugar

1. Roast coriander and cumin till light brown.
2. Grind all the ingredients of the red curry paste and the roasted ingredients using the water in which the chillies were soaked, to a very fine paste.
3. Heat the oil in a large pan, add the red curry paste and fry for a 2-3 minutes on low heat.
4. Add chicken and stir fry for 5-6 minutes on medium heat.
5. Add 2 tbsp of coconut milk.
6. Add the rest of the coconut milk, fish sauce, soya sauce and lemon leaves.
7. Cook covered on low heat for 7-8 minutes till the chicken is almost tender.
8. Add vegetables, salt and sugar to taste. Add chopped basil leaves and ½ cup water. Boil for 5-6 minutes till chicken and vegetables are cooked. Serve hot garnished with a red chilli flower or slices with steamed rice or noodles.

Note: You can use any vegetables of your choice.

The red curry paste can be made extra and store in an airtight container (for upto 1 month). Alternatively, freeze for upto 3 months. To obtain a bright red curry paste, use red Kashmiri chillies as for as possible.

Green Curry with Chicken and Aubergine

Although the combination is a little odd but it tastes delicious.

Picture on page 40   *Serves 5-6*

150 gms aubergine (preferably) use the small green variety, however the ordinary purple one can also be used
3 tbsp oil
7 tbsp green curry paste (see page 17)
300 gms chicken - boneless or with bones - cut into 1" pieces
2½ cups coconut milk
1 tsp salt
1 tsp sugar/gur
2 tbsp fish sauce (optional)
½ tsp soya sauce
2-3 lemon leaves (nimbu ke patte)
2-3 green/red chillies - slit long for garnishing

1. Heat oil in a pan. Add green curry paste. Fry for 2-3 minutes.
2. Add chicken and stir fry for 4-5 minutes.
3. Add 1 cup coconut milk, lower heat and simmer for 4-5 minutes or till chicken is nearly done.
4. Add salt, sugar, fish sauce, soya sauce, lemon leaves, brinjal and the rest of the coconut milk. Boil. Cover and cook on low heat till brinjal and chicken are well cooked.
5. Garnish with sliced green chillies (long thin slices), basil leaves and serve hot with boiled/ steamed rice.

Crispy Chicken in Shell

Serves 3-4

Picture on page 3

250 gms chicken- cut into ½" flat pieces
5- 6 cashewnuts (kaju), a few pieces of chopped pineapple (6-7, ½" pieces)

MARINADE
1 egg
2 tbsp finely chopped lemon grass (see page 11)
1 tbsp chopped coriander, 1 tsp chopped garlic
2 dry red chillies, 1 tbsp white wine, ½ tsp pepper, ½ tsp salt
2 tbsp cornflour, 1" stick cinnamon (dalchini)

BATTER
¼ cup roasted rice powder (grind raw rice in a mixer to a powder and roast in a kadhai till light golden), ¼ tsp soya sauce, ½ cup cornflour, ¼ cup chilled water
1 tbsp oil, ½ tsp red chilli flakes, ½ tsp salt

TO STIR FRY
1 onion- cut into 8 pieces, 15- 20 basil leaves
1 tbsp tomato ketchup, 1 tsp honey, ¼ cup chopped pineapple
a pinch of salt & pepper, or to taste

1. Cut chicken into flat pieces.
2. Churn all ingredients of marinade in a mixer to a paste.
3. Transfer the marinade to a flat bowl and add chicken to the prepared marinade. Keep aside for 5- 6 hours.
4. Mix all ingredients of batter in a bowl. Mix well and keep aside for 30 minutes. Mix again after 30 minutes.
5. Heat oil in a kadhai. Dip each pieces of marinated chicken mix well so that a thick coating covers the chicken, covering on all the sides. Immediately deep fry till golden brown.

6. Deep fry the cashewnuts for few seconds without the batter in the same oil.
7. Heat 1 tsp oil. Add onion and cook till soft.
8. Add basil leaves and mix well.
9. Add honey, vinegar, tomato ketchup, salt, pepper and stir fry for 2 minutes.

10. Add fried chicken and chopped pineapple, mix well and serve hot in a hollowed warmed pineapple shell or in a bowl.

Spicy Honey Chicken

Picture on page 40   *Serves 4*

250 gm chicken breast boneless - cut into 1½" pieces
½ cup cornflour - approx.
2-3 dry, red chillies - broken into bits
2 tsp garlic paste
2 tbsp spring onions - white part finely chopped and greens cut into 1" pieces
2½ tbsp tomato ketchup
1½- 2 tbsp soya sauce, 2 tsp honey
1 tbsp fish sauce
1 tsp oyster sauce
1 tbsp lemon rind (see page 11)

MARINADE
2 eggs
½ tsp salt
½ tsp ajinomoto (optional), 1 tbsp cornflour, 1 tbsp oil

1. Mix all ingredients of marinade in a bowl.
2. Add chicken. Mix well and keep aside for 1 hour.
3. Add ½ cup cornflour to the marinated chicken. Mix well.
4. Heat oil in a kadhai and deep fry the chicken pieces on medium heat till crisp and cook. Drain and keep aside.
5. Heat 2 tbsp oil in a wok. Reduce heat. Add dry, red chillies and stir. Add garlic paste. Stir for a few seconds.
6. Add finely chopped white part of spring onions, tomato ketchup, soya sauce honey, fish sauce, oyster sauce and rind of 1 lemon. Saute for a few seconds.
7. Add the crispy fried chicken and stir-fry ensuring that each piece is coated with the sauce. Mix in the greens of spring onions. Check salt and pepper. Remove from fire. Serve hot.

Masaman Curry

This curry can be made with chicken or mutton. For a vegetarian version, use paneer or bean curd. It has a rich, sweet and spicy flavour. Serve with boiled rice.

Serves 4

400 gms chicken - cut into small pieces (can be boneless or with bones)
3-4 tbsp oil
3½ cups coconut milk
6-8 tbsp heaped masaman curry paste (see page 18)
½ tsp haldi powder (optional) - gives a better colour if used
3 tbsp fish sauce
1-2 tsp sugar/gur (adjust to taste)
5 tbsp tamarind juice (soak 1 lemon sized ball of imli in hot water and strain)
1 tbsp finely chopped lemon grass (use only stem, see page 11)
1" cinnamon stick (dalchini)
2 medium potatoes - cut into bite size even pieces
1 large onion - cut into wedges & leaves separated
1½ tsp salt, or to taste
50 gms (½ cup) roasted peanuts (moongphali)
3- 4 lemon leaves (nimbu ke patte), optional

1. Heat oil. Add masaman curry paste and ½ tsp haldi. Fry for 2-3 minutes till aromatic and leaves oil.
2. Add chicken. Fry for 5-6 minutes. Add potatoes and onion. Fry for 2-3 minutes.
3. Add coconut milk and lemon leaves. Mix well.
4. Add all other ingredients except roasted peanuts and cook covered on low heat for 6-8 minutes or till chicken and potatoes are fully cooked.
5. Add roasted peanuts. Cook for another 3-4 minutes and serve hot with rice.

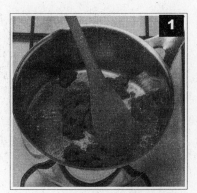
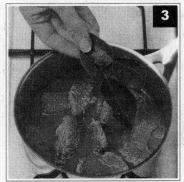

Chicken Yellow Curry

Serves 4

250 gm chicken- cut into thin flat pieces
1 small cauliflower or broccoli (250 gms) - cut into small florets
50 gms babycorn - each cut into 2 pieces, lengthwise
¼ cup chopped bamboo shoots (optional)
yellow curry paste (see page 18, make full quantity)
1 egg
4 tbsp oil
1" pieces of ginger - peeled & sliced thinly
2 tbsp roasted peanuts (moongphali) - roughly crushed
1 vegetable seasoning cube (use maggi or knorr)
2 cups coconut milk mixed with 1 tbsp cornflour
1 tbsp finely chopped lemon grass (use only stem, see page 11)
5-6 lemon leaves (nimbu ke patte)
15 basil leaves - chopped or 2 tbsp chopped coriander leaves
½ tsp brown sugar or regular sugar
1 cup water

1. Mix chicken with egg and ½ tsp salt.
2. Heat 4 tbsp oil in a kadhai. Add egg and chicken and stir fry for 2-3 minutes.
3. Add yellow curry paste. Fry for 3- 4 minutes on low heat.
4. Add ginger, peanuts and seasoning cube. Mix well for 2 minutes.
5. Add coconut milk, lemon leaves, chopped lemon grass and chopped basil leaves.
6. Add water. Simmer on low heat for 5-7 minutes till the vegetables are tender.
7. Add salt and sugar to taste. Boil for 1 to 2 minutes. Serve hot garnished with a red chilli flower or slices with steamed rice or noodles.

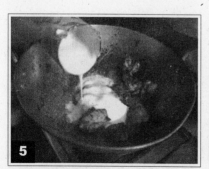
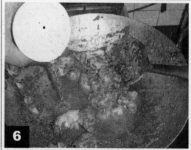

Chicken with Basil & Chillies

This quick & easy semi-dry dish is an excellent introduction to Thai cuisine. Deep frying basil leaves add a different dimension to the dish.

Serves 5-6

500 gm chicken, boneless or with bones - cut into bite size pieces
5 tbsp oil
6-8 flakes garlic - chopped
4 dried, red chillies - whole and 6-8 fresh green chillies - chopped
4 tbsp red or 4 tbsp green curry paste (see page 17)
2 tbsp fish sauce (optional)
2 tsp soya sauce (adjust to taste)
1 tsp sugar/gur
10-12 basil leaves

GARNISHING
20 basil leaves - deep fried (optional)

1. Heat oil in a wok or frying pan.
2. Add garlic and chillies (red whole and chopped green chillies). Fry for 1-2 minutes till garlic is golden brown.
3. Add curry paste and fry well.
4. Add chicken. Stir fry till it changes colour. Cover, lower heat and cook till tender.
5. Add fish sauce, soya sauce, sugar and basil leaves. Mix well. Stir fry for another 5-6 minutes. Add 4 tbsp water. Mix well for a minute. Remove from fire.
6. For garnishing, fry basil leaves. Before frying basil leaves make sure they are absolutely dry. Deep fry in hot oil for about 30-40 seconds, lift out of oil and drain on kitchen paper.
7. Garnish the chicken with red chillies and fried basil leaves.

Note: No salt has been added as the salt in fish sauce and soya sauce is enough. However taste it and add as required.

Peanut Chicken

This curry is a little on the sweet side, delicious with a lovely peanut & coconut flavour. Serve with boiled/steamed rice.

Serves 3- 4

300 gms chicken - cut into small pieces (boneless)
½ cup roasted salted peanuts (moongphali), 1 tsp salt
3 tbsp butter, 8-10 flakes garlic - crushed
2 onion - chopped, ½ tsp red chilli powder
2 tsp dhania powder, 2 tsp jeera powder (cumin powder)
2 cup coconut milk, ready made or fresh (given below)
4 tbsp fish sauce (optional)
6 lemon leaves (optional)
2 tbsp oil, 1 tsp sugar, 1½ tsp lemon juice, 1 tsp soya sauce

1. Grind peanuts with the salt to a rough powder.
2. Heat 3 tbsp butter in a heavy bottomed small pan or kadhai. Add crushed garlic. Saute till it starts to change colour. Add onions, cook till soft. Reduce heat.
3. Add chicken and stir fry for 5-6 minutes.
4. Add ½ tsp red chilli powder, dhania powder, jeera powder. Add only ½ cup coconut milk. Boil, stirring. Cook on low heat for 3 minutes, stirring constantly.
5. Add crushed peanuts, fish sauce, lemon leaves, ½ tsp sugar, 1½ tsp lemon juice, 1 tsp Soya sauce and remaining ½ cup coconut milk. Boil. Simmer gently for 5 minutes, stirring occasionally to prevent it from sticking to the pan. Serve hot.

Chicken Stirred with Cashewnuts

Picture on page 57   *Serves 2*

200 gms chicken, boneless - cut into small strips
6-8 mushrooms - each cut into 2 pieces
1 spring onion - cut bulb into 4 pieces and green into 1" long pieces
2 tbsp oil, 1 tbsp chopped garlic, 1" piece ginger - chopped
½ tsp salt & ½ tsp crushed peppercorns (adjust to taste)
½ tsp sugar, 1 tbsp fish sauce, 1 tbsp soya sauce
½ green and ½ red capsicum - cut into 1" squares
¼ cup freshly roasted or fried cashewnuts, 4 fresh red chillies - slit lengthwise

1. Heat oil in a pan/kadhai. Fry garlic and white part of onion till onion turns light brown. Add ginger. Stir.
2. Add chicken and mushrooms. Fry for 4-5 minutes.
3. Reduce heat. Add salt, pepper, sugar, fish sauce, soya sauce, green and red capsicums, cashewnuts and red chillies. Saute for 2-3 minutes. Serve hot.

Stir Fried Sweet & Sour Chicken/ Fish/Pork/Prawns

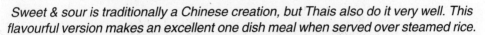

Sweet & sour is traditionally a Chinese creation, but Thais also do it very well. This flavourful version makes an excellent one dish meal when served over steamed rice.

Serves 4

200 gm boneless chicken - cut into small pieces or fish - cut into 1" pieces or pork - sliced thinly or prawns of 1" in size
3 tbsp oil
5-6 large flakes garlic - chopped, 1 medium onion - sliced
2 tbsp vinegar
2 tbsp fish sauce
1 medium tomato - cut into 1-1½" long pieces
1 medium capsicum - cut into 1-1½" long pieces
1 medium cucumber - cut into 1-1½" long pieces
2 tsp cornflour
4 tbsp tomato sauce
½ tsp salt
1 tbsp sugar - adjust to taste
½ - 1 tsp pepper - adjust to taste
½ cup tinned pineapple - cut into chunks

GARNISHING
2 spring onions - sliced diagonally into 1½" length
some fresh coriander leaves

1. Heat 3 tbsp oil. Add garlic. Fry till brown.
2. Add chicken or pork. Stri fry for 3-4 minutes.
3. Add onion. Cover and cook on low heat till chicken/pork is tender. If using prawns or fish this is not required as they cook very fast.
4. Add vegetables and if using prawns or fish. Fry for 3-4 minutes or till they are crunchy tender.
5. Add all seasonings. Mix well.
6. Dissolve cornflour in ¼ cup water. Add. Cook for 4-5 minutes. Add pineapple. Mix well. Serve garnished with spring onions and coriander with steamed/boiled rice.

Prawns in Red Curry

Picture on facing page   *Serves 4*

250 gms prawns - use 2"-3" long prawns shelled but with their tails intact. However, if these are not available you can use small ones
½ cup red curry paste (see page 17)
2 cups coconut milk, 1 tbsp fish sauce
½ tsp salt, (optional), ½ tsp sugar or gur
4-5 cherry tomatoes or 2 medium tomatoes - remove pulp and cut into 1" pieces
1 tsp lemon juice
3-4 green/red chillies & basil leaves for garnishing

1. Heat 2 tbsp oil. Add curry paste. Fry for 2 minutes till aromatic and leaves oil. Add ¾ cup coconut milk. Boil, stirring constantly. Simmer for 5-7 minutes.
2. Add fish sauce, salt and sugar. Add the rest of the coconut milk. Boil for 3-4 minutes. Add prawns and tomatoes. Cook for 4-5 minutes till prawns are cooked (turn pink) and curry becomes thick. Add lemon juice. Mix.
3. Garnish with chopped chillies and coriander leaves. Serve hot.

Fish Curry

Serves 3-4   *Picture on opposite page*

300 gms fish - cleaned & washed and cut into small (¾") pieces
3-4 tbsp red curry paste or 2-3 tbsp green curry paste (page 17)
2 cups ready-made coconut milk or mix 1 packet coconut powder (maggi) mixed
with 1½ cups milk and ½ cup water
1 tbsp fish sauce, 3-4 lemon leaves (nimbu ke patte)
½ tsp salt, 1 tsp sugar/gur (optional)
¼ - ½ cup basil leaves - shredded
3-4 chillies (green or red) - sliced

1. Heat 2 tbsp oil. Add curry paste. Fry for 2 minutes on low heat.
2. Add ½ cup coconut milk. Cook till nearly dry and fragrant.
3. Add fish sauce, lemon leaves, salt and sugar. Add the rest of the coconut milk. Give it one boil.
4. Add fish and basil. Cover and cook for 5-6 minutes, till fish is well done.
5. Garnish with sliced chillies and serve hot with steamed/boiled rice.

Note : Instead of fish, prawns, crabs, paneer and mixed vegetables can be used.

Garlic Fish

Instead of Fish; Prawns, Chicken, Paneer or Mushrooms can be used.

Serves 2-3

250 gms boneless fish - cut into 2" pieces
1 tbsp vinegar or lemon juice
1 tsp garlic paste, 1 tsp ginger paste
1 tbsp chopped ginger, 2 tbsp chopped garlic
1 tsp red chilli paste (grind 2-3 dry red chillies with 4 tbsp water to a paste)
½ cup (2-3) chopped spring onions
1¼ tsp salt, 1 tsp pepper
2 tbsp fish sauce
1 tbsp chopped coriander

1. Mix together lemon juice, garlic and ginger paste. Marinate fish in it for 1-2 hours.
2. Heat 2 tbsp oil in a pan/wok. Add chopped ginger and garlic. Fry for 1-2 minutes.
3. Add red chilli paste. Fry for 1 minute.
4. Add spring onions, salt, pepper, fish sauce and fish. Cook for 2 minutes.
5. Cover, lower heat and cook for another 2-3 minutes.
6. Increase heat (check if tender), dry. Serve hot, garnished with chopped coriander.

Batter fried Prawns in Lemon Sauce

Instead of prawns, boneless fish or boneless chicken can be used.

Picture on backcover   *Serves 4*

100 gms small prawns or chicken or fish

BATTER
2 tbsp maida (plain flour), 1 tbsp cornflour, 1 egg
½ tsp ginger paste, ½ tsp garlic paste
½ tsp salt, ½ tsp pepper, 1 tsp red chilli paste
oil for frying

SAUCE
2 cups water, 4-5 tbsp honey - adjust to taste
5 tbsp sugar - adjust to taste, ½ cup fresh lemon juice
1 tsp grated ginger, 1 tsp crushed garlic
½ tsp salt, 3-4 lemon leaves, 3 tbsp cornflour
a few drops (1-2 drops) of lemon yellow food colouring
1 spring onion - sliced diagonally alongwith the green part
some fresh chopped coriander leaves

1. Mix all ingredients under batter. Mix in prawns/chicken.
2. Heat oil. Drop prawns in hot oil.
3. Fry till golden brown for 2- 3 minutes on medium heat. Keep aside.
4. To prepare the sauce, mix all ingredients except the last two — spring onions and coriander.
5. Boil till sugar dissolves and sauce turns thick.
6. Add fried chicken/prawns. Add spring onions and coriander leaves.
7. Give 1-2 boils and serve hot.

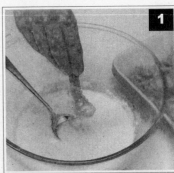
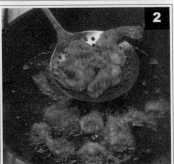

Stir Fried Prawns with Vegetables

Serves 3-4

10-12 dried, whole red chillies
200 gm small prawns or 3-4" long prawns - shelled, with tail intact and deveined
10 babycorns
10 mushrooms (fresh or dried)
1 tbsp chopped garlic
3 tbsp fish sauce, 1 tsp soya sauce
¼ tsp salt, 6-8 peppercorns - crushed
¼ tsp red chilli paste or powder

1. Slice mushrooms into big pieces, cutting each into 2 or 3 pieces.
2. Cut babycorns lengthwise into two pieces and then cut into two smaller pieces.
3. Heat 2 tbsp oil in a wok/frying pan. Add garlic. Fry for 1 minute.
4. Add salt, red chilli paste/powder. Fry for 1 minute.
5. Add prawns and babycorns. Fry for 2 minutes.
6. Add mushrooms, soya sauce and fish sauce. Cook for 2 minutes.
7. Serve garnished with green chillies and crushed peppercorns.

Note: You can use 200 gm boneless chicken - cut into small instead of prawns.

Deveining of Prawns

Prawns in Garlic Sauce

Picture on page 58   *Serves 6*

12 prawns - shelled & deveined
oil for frying

MARINADE
1 egg - lightly beaten
1 tsp salt, ½-1 tsp sugar
¼ tsp ajinomoto (optional)
1 tsp oil
¼ tsp pepper powder
¼ cup cornflour

SAUCE
2 tbsp garlic paste (10-20 flakes of garlic- crushed to a paste)
2 tbsp oil
3 tsp soya sauce, 2 tbsp tomato ketchup
1¼ cups water
½ tsp white pepper, ¾ tsp salt
2 tbsp cornflour mixed with ½ cup water
a pinch of sugar
¼ tsp ajinomoto (optional)

1. Beat egg lightly with salt, sugar, ajinomoto, oil, pepper and cornflour.
2. Add prawns to this mixture, stir and leave to marinate for 30 minutes.
3. Heat plenty of oil in wok. Drain off excess marinade from the prawns and fry them for 2-3 minutes till golden brown.
4. Drain well and place on paper towel.
5. To prepare the sauce, heat oil and fry the garlic on low heat till it starts to change it's colour.
6. Add tomato ketchup, pepper, salt and soya sauce. Cook for 1 minute.

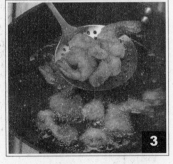

7. Add sugar and ajinomoto.
8. Add water. Bring to a boil and simmer for 2 minutes.
9. Add cornflour paste, stirring all the time, until the sauce thickens. Remove from heat.
10. Add the fried prawns and heat through. Serve hot.

Thai Flat Noodles

Serves 2   *Picture on page 1*

200 gm flat noodles, preferably rice noodles - break into 4"- 5" length
½ cup shredded basil leaves or tulsi
1 tsp garlic paste, 4 tbsp crushed peanuts (moongphali)
3 tsp tomato ketchup
¼ tsp salt or to taste

1. Boil 6-8 cups water. Add noodles to boiling water and stir with a fork. Let noodles be in hot water for 1-2 minutes. Drain. Wash with cold water and strain. Keep in the strainer for 15 minutes for all the water to drain out. Sprinkle 1 tbsp oil and mix.
2. Spread a muslin cloth on a large tray. Put the noodles on the cloth for ½ hour to dry out.
3. Heat 4 tbsp oil. Add garlic paste, cook till golden. Add peanuts and basil leaves.
4. Add boiled noodles. Add tomato ketchup and salt.
5. Mix well with the help of 2 forks. Fry for 2-3 minutes. Serve hot.

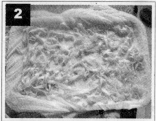

Pad Thai (Flat Noodles with Vegetables)

Serves 4-5

4 cups boiled (200 gms) noodles, preferably, flat noodles
2 large carrots - cut into diagonal slices and then into strips of ¼" thickness
1 cup bean sprouts with long shoots - optional
1 stalk lemon grass - very finely chopped (see page 11)
6-8 lemon leaves (nimbu ke patte) - shredded
10 -12 garlic flakes - crushed (1½ tbsp)
1 onion - shredded or thinly sliced
1½ tsp salt
1 tsp soya sauce, 4-5 tbsp lemon juice
4 tbsp roasted peanuts - coarsely ground
5 tbsp oil

SUGAR SYRUP
3 tbsp sugar mixed with ¼ cup water and boiled for a minute

RED CHILLI PASTE
3-4 dry red chillies - deseed and ground to a paste with 1 tbsp water

1. Boil 8-10 cups water with 2 tsp salt and 1 tbsp oil. Add noodles to boiling water. Remove from fire. Let noodles be in hot water for 1 minute. Strain. Rinse in cold water. Drain and keep aside. Keep aside in the strainer for all the water to drain out.
2. Prepare sugar syrup and keep aside.
3. Wash sprouts in several changes of water. Leave in the strainer.
4. Heat 5 tbsp oil in a non stick wok or pan. Reduce heat. Add garlic. Stir. Add red chilli paste. Fry for about 1 minute.
5. Add lemon grass, onions and bean sprouts. Fry for 2 minutes till onions turn soft.
6. Add carrots and lemon leaves. Mix. Stir fry for 2 minutes. Reduce heat.
7. Add noodles. Do not mix. Add 2½ tsp salt, sugar syrup, lemon juice, soya sauce and 4 tbsp peanuts. Increase heat and mix well using 2 spoons.
8. Serve hot sprinkled with some roasted and crushed peanuts.

Sticky Rice

Sticky rice is easier to eat with chopsticks! It's a little sweet because of the honey added to it. Use new rice because the grains stick to each other on cooking.

Serves 6

1½ cups uncooked rice (short grained new rice)
2 tbsp oil
1 onion - sliced, 2 flakes garlic - crushed
2 spring onions - chop white and green part separately
2 green chillies - chopped
½ cup peas (matar)
½ tsp jeera powder (cumin powder), ½ tsp dhania powder (ground coriander)
1 tsp saunf (fennel seeds) - crushed
1 tsp salt, ½ tsp pepper

MIX TOGETHER
3 cups veg stock or 3 cups of water mixed with 1 vegetable seasoning cube (maggi or knorr)
2 tbsp honey
2 tbsp soya sauce

1. Wash and soak rice. Keep aside.
2. Mix all the ingredients written under mix together in a bowl. Keep aside.
3. Heat oil in a large deep pan, add sliced onion and garlic and stir-fry for 4-5 minutes or until onion is soft.
4. Add white part of spring onion, green chillies and peas.
5. Add jeera powder, dhania powder, crushed saunf, salt and pepper. Stir-fry for 1 minute.
6. Drain rice and add to the pan. Stir for 3-4 minutes on low heat.
7. Add stock-honey mixture and green of spring onion. Stir and bring to a boil.
8. Reduce heat and cook covered for 10 minutes or until rice is done and the water gets absorbed. Serve hot.

Tip: Do not use old rice. The newer the rice, the more sticky it becomes when cooked. To see if the rice is old or new, shake the packet of rice. If powder stick to the sides, it is old rice.

Bajang (rice)

Serves 6

3 cups rice - soak rice for 1 hour in some water, drain
1½" stick dalchini (cinnamon), seeds of 2 moti illaichi (black cardamom)
2 dry red chillies, 1½ cup boiled peas (matar)
4 tbsp black bean sauce, 2 tbsp soya sauce
2 onions - chopped, 1 lemon grass- tied into a knot
1 tsp pepper, 3¾ tsp salt, 2-3 tsp chopped coriander, 2 cups coconut milk

1. Heat 6 tbsp oil in a saucepan/patila, add dalchini, moti illaichi and dry red chilli. Wait for 1 minute. Add onion, stir fry till golden.
3. Add rice and all the other ingredients, mix well for 2-3 minutes.
4. Add 4 cups water. Cover and cook for ½ hour on medium flame.
5. Remove lemon grass before serving. Serve hot.

Masaman Curried Rice

Delicious aromatic rice which can be had plain without any other dish. It is a complete meal by itself almost like a masala vegetable biryani.

Picture on backcover   *Serves 4-5*

1 cup basmati rice (soaked for 10-15 minutes)
Some Masaman paste (given on page 18)
½ cup french beans - diced
½ cup carrots - diced, ½ capsicum - diced
2 tsp coconut powder (maggi) mixed with ½ cup milk
2 tsp salt, ½ tsp haldi powder
2 stalks lemon grass - tie into a knot, discard when rice is ready
3 tbsp lemon juice, 4 tbsp oil
1 cup coconut milk OR use half packet coconut powder (maggi) mixed with
½ cup milk

1. Heat oil in a kadahi or a saucepan (patila) with a well fitted lid. Add masaman curry paste. Fry till aromatic and leaves oil.
2. Mix 2 tsp coconut powder with ½ cup milk.
3. Add this coconut milk, in the kadahi, cook till nearly dry.
4. Add vegetables, stir fry for a minute.
5. Add salt, haldi, lemon juice, lemon grass, 1 cup coconut milk, 1 cup water and soaked rice.
6. Give one boil. Cook covered for 5-8 minutes or till all the water has dried and the rice is cooked. Discard lemon grass.
7. Serve hot garnished with fresh coriander, lemon wedges and tomato slices.

Chicken Masaman Rice

Delicious aromatic biryani which can be had plain without any side dish. A complete meal in itself. Must not miss it, try it right away!

Serves 4

2 cups basmati rice - soaked for 30 minutes in water
500 gms chicken, with or without bones - cut into 8 small pieces
4 tsp salt, 1 tsp haldi powder (turmeric powder)
5 cups ready-made coconut milk OR 12 tbsp coconut powder (2 packets of maggi coconut powder) mixed with 3 cups water and 2 cups milk
3½ tbsp lemon juice, 7 tbsp oil

PASTE (makes ½ cup approx.)
10 dried, red chillies, rind of 1 lemon (see page 11)
2 onions - chopped
12-14 flakes of garlic, 4 tsp chopped ginger
2 tbsp cumin seeds (jeera), 2 tsp saunf (fennel)
2" stick dalchini (cinnamon), seeds of 4 moti illaichi (brown cardamom)
¼ tsp grated jaiphal (nutmeg)
4 tbsp saboot dhania (coriander seeds)
4 laung (cloves), 8 saboot kali mirch (black peppercorns)

1. For the paste, roast all ingredients of the paste in a kadhai/wok for 5 minutes or till fragrant. See picture.
2. Grind to a fine paste. Use little water if needed.
3. Use coconut milk or mix one packet coconut milk powder (maggi) with 3 cups of water and 2 cups milk. Keep coconut milk aside.
4. Heat 7 tbsp oil in a deep pan with a well fitted lid. Add the chicken and bhuno for 10 minutes on medium flame till chicken gets golden brown from various sides.
5. Add prepared paste. Fry for about 3 minutes or till it leaves oil.
6. Reduce heat, add ½ cup of prepared coconut milk. Cook till nearly dry for about 2- 3 minutes.
7. Add salt, haldi, remaining coconut milk, and the soaked rice. Mix well gently.
8. Give one boil. Reduce heat and cook covered on very low heat for 10-12 minutes or till all the water has dried and the rice is cooked. Shut of the flame.
9. Sprinkle lemon juice, mix gently with a fork.
10. Remove from fire and transfer to a serving plate. Separate the grains with a fork. Serve garnished with lemon wedges and tomato slices.

Peanut Fried Rice

Fried rice flavoured with peanuts.

Serves 3-4

1½ cups uncooked rice
3 tbsp oil
4 flakes garlic - crushed (optional)
2 green chillies - chopped finely
2 green onions - chopped till the greens, keep greens separate
1 tsp salt, 1 tsp pepper, ¼ tsp ajinomoto (optional)
½ tsp soya sauce (according to the colour desired), 1 tsp vinegar (optional)
½ tsp tomato ketchup

GRIND TOGETHER TO A PASTE
3 tbsp roasted peanuts
5½ tbsp milk

FOR GARNISHING
2 tbsp roasted peanuts - roughly crushed on a chakla belan

1. To boil rice, clean and wash 1½ cups rice. Soak rice for 10 minutes.
2. Boil 6 cups of water with 2 tsp salt. Add rice. Cook, uncovered, over a medium flame, stirring occasionally, until the rice is just tender but not **overcooked.** Drain the rice and let it stand in the strainer for sometime. Fluff with a fork. Spread on a tray and cool under a fan to separate the rice grains.
3. Grind all ingredients of paste to a smooth paste.
4. Chop spring onions till the greens, keep white and green separately.
5. Heat oil. Stir fry garlic, green chillies and white of onions.
6. Add peanut paste. Mix. Reduce heat, add salt, pepper and ajinomoto, soya sauce, vinegar and tomato ketchup. Mix.
7. Add boiled rice and green portion of spring onions. Mix and stir fry the rice for 2 minutes with the help of 2 forks. Remove from fire.
8. Serve hot garnished with crushed roasted peanuts.

Glass Noodles with Sesame Paste

Glass noodles are thin long translucent noodles. In the absence of these the regular noodles or rice seviyaan can be used.

Serves 6

100 gms glass noodles or rice seviyaan
2 tbsp oil
3 spring onions - cut into rings, till the greens, keep white separate

SESAME PASTE (GRIND ALL TOGETHER)
3 tbsp sesame seeds (til) - soak for 10 minutes in 5 tbsp hot milk and 2 tbsp water
and then grind to a paste
½ tsp red chilli powder or to taste, ¾ tsp salt
4 flakes garlic - finely chopped
1½ tbsp soya sauce
½ tsp sugar

1. Cut white spring onion into rings till the greens.
2. In a large pan, boil 8 cups water with 1 tsp salt and 1 tsp oil. Remove from fire. Add noodles to hot water. Cover & keep aside for 5 minutes in hot water. Drain.
3. Wash with cold water several times. Strain. Leave them in the strainer for 15-20 minutes, turning them upside down, once after about 10 minutes to ensure complete drying. Apply 1 tsp oil on the noodles and spread on a large tray. Dry the noodles under a fan for 15-20 minutes. Keep aside till further use.
4. Grind all ingredients of sesame paste to a smooth paste.
5. Heat oil in a pan, remove from fire. Swirl the pan to coat the bottom of the pan nicely with oil. Add white portion of spring onions, stir for a minute.
6. Add prepared sesame paste mixture, mix well and stir for 2 minutes on low heat.
7. Add boiled noodles, mix well. Add spring onion greens. Mix & remove from fire.

Desserts

Fried Ice Cream Ball

A wonderful combination of hot and cold. Remember to use a well set, hard ice cream for this dessert. Should be made well in advance, so that it is firm at the time of frying. These are oriental desserts which go well with a Chinese meal also.

Serves 8-10

1 hard family brick (1 lt) vanilla ice cream - scooped to make big balls, about 7-8
12 slices of fresh bread - broken into small pieces
6 tbsp orange marmalade or any other jam
¾ cup desiccated coconut (coconut powder)

COATING (MIX TOGETHER)
½ cup rice flour (grind some raw rice in mixer grinder and sift to get fine powder),
rice flour is available at chakkis too
¼ tsp cinnamon powder (dalchini powder)

1. Scoop out big balls of hard ice cream and keep in the freezer.
2. Grind half of the bread at a time in the mixer for just 2-3 seconds to get coarse bread crumbs. Remove from mixer to a big bowl. Grind the remaining bread and put all in the bowl.
3. To the bread crumbs, add jam and coconut powder. Mix gently.
4. Put the rice flour in a separate bowl. Mix cinnamon powder in it.
5. Take a scoop of ice cream and make it into a round ball by rolling it between your hands. Immediately put in the bread bowl and picking up the bread crumbs, coat the ball nicely with bread. Keep on coating till it can take no more bread.
6. Roll in rice flour and cinnamon. Roll once again in bread crumbs. Finally roll in rice flour and then keep in the freezer to get hard. (I generally put them in a box and freeze overnight.) Keep in the freezer till serving time.
7. At serving time, heat 1½ cups oil in a kadhai for frying. Do not fill the kadhai with oil. Put one ball at a time in hot oil. Change side after 30 seconds. Do not touch it immediately. Fry turning sides till crisp and golden. Remove on paper napkins to absorb excess oil. Serve whole or cut into half with a sharp knife. Top with a little coconut powder if you like.

Date Pancakes

Serves 8

½ cup cornflour, ½ cup plain flour (maida)
¼ cup milk or slightly more
2 tsp melted butter, 2 tbsp powdered sugar

FILLING
300 gm dates (khajoor) - deseeded and finely chopped (2 cups)
2 tbsp sesame seeds (til) - toasted on a tawa (griddle) till golden
2 tbsp butter, ½ cup water

TO SERVE
vanilla ice-cream
some desiccated coconut (coconut powder)

1. Sift the cornflour and plain flour together. Add butter and sugar. Add just enough milk and knead to a firm, smooth dough. Cover and keep aside for 15 minutes.
2. For the filling, toast sesame seeds in a non stick pan or a tawa till golden. Remove from pan and keep aside. In the same pan melt butter. Add dates and stir for 2 minutes. Add water and cook on low heat for about 2-3 minutes, till a little pulpy and slightly dry. Remove from fire and mix in the toasted sesame seeds. Keep filling aside.
3. Make 8 small balls from the dough. Roll out each ball to a thin chappati.
4. Spread some filling on half of it. Dot the edges with water all around. Fold over to get a semi circle. Press the edges to stick together. Make all pancakes in the same way and keep covered with a cling wrap till serving time.
5. To serve heat a cup of oil in a frying pan and gently slide the stuffed pancake. Shallow fry on medium heat until crisp, turning sides. Cut into two pieces and top with desiccated coconut. Serve with vanilla ice cream.

Coconut Custard

Picture on page 93   *Serves 8*

2¼ cups coconut milk, 7 tbsp sugar or to taste
4 tbsp cornflour dissolved in ½ cup water
1½ tsp cinnamon powder, a drop of green colour

1. Heat coconut milk and sugar in a saucepan to a boil.
2. Add cornflour paste and cook, stirring till it starts to thicken and coats the back of a spoon. Add colour. Mix well. Remove from fire immediately.
3. Add cinnamon powder. Serve.

Dates on Fire

Steamed date cakes prepared in a pressure cooker flambed on the serving table. You can make this cake in the oven also. See note given below.

Picture on page 93   *Serves 4*

½ cup deseeded and chopped dates
¼ cup water, ¼ tsp soda - bi- carb (mitha soda)
50 gm (¼ cup) white butter
½ cup brown sugar
¼ cup maida, ¼ cup cornflour
1 tsp baking powder, 1 egg, 1 tbsp milk

MIXED SPICE CRUSH TOGETHER
1" stick cinnamon (dalchini)
2 cloves (laung)

TO FLAMBE (OPTIONAL)
some desiccated coconut, 3 tbsp rum or brandy sauce

1. Soak finely chopped dates in ¼ cup water in a bowl. Sprinkle ¼ tsp soda on them. Mix well and keep aside for 15 minutes.
2. Grind dates to a puree a keep aside.
3. Beat butter with brown sugar till fluffy. Add the date paste to butter sugar mixture.
4. Sift maida, cornflour and baking powder.
5. Beat egg lightly.
6. Add maida mixture and egg to the date mixture.
7. Add the mixed spice and beat well.
8. Add 1 tbsp milk to get a soft dropping consisting. Beat well.
9. Grease 4 small steel katoris a cake moulds. Pour cake mixture in them.

10. Take a pressure cooker. Put ½" high water in it. Place the "jaali" or the perforated steel plate of the cooker in it. (No water in the cooker !) Place the katoris on the jaali. Close the cooker. Remove the weight of the cooker. Place cooker on fire. After 2 minutes reduce heat to minimum. (It is better to put a tawa on low heat and then place the cooker on the tawa. This reduces the heat further). Keep cooker on fire on 30 minutes. Remove from fire. Open the cooker after 5-7 minutes.
11. At serving time put the cakes on a platter sprinkle some desiccated coconut.
12. If you want to flambe the cake then take 1-2 tbsp rum or brandy in a kadahi and heat it on fire. After 1-2 minutes, when it catches fire, pour immediately on the cakes. Serve immediately with flames on the cake.

Note: You can bake the cakes at 180° C for 20 minutes in a preheated oven.

Glossary of Indian Names/Terms

Hindi or English names as used in India	English names as used in USA/UK/ Other countries
Ajwain	Carom seeds
Aloo	Potatoes
Badaam	Almonds
Baingan	Eggplant, aubergine
Basmati rice	Fragrant Indian rice
Besan	Gram flour
Bhutta	Corn
Capsicum	Bell peppers
Chaawal, Chawal	Rice
Chilli powder	Red chilli powder, Cayenne pepper
Cornflour	Corn starch
Coriander, fresh	Cilantro
Cream	Heavy whipping cream
Curd	Yogurt
Dahi	Yogurt
Dalchini	Cinnamon
Dhania powder	Ground coriander seeds
Dhania saboot	Coriander seeds
Essence	Extract
French beans	Green beans
Gajar	Carrots
Gobhi	Cauliflower
Haldi	Turmeric powder
Hara Dhania	Cilantro, Coriander
Hari Gobhi	Broccoli
Hari Mirchi	Green hot peppers, green chillies, serrano peppers
Illaichi	Cardamom
Imli	Tamarind
Jaiphal	Nutmeg
Javetri	Mace
Jeera Powder	Ground cumin seeds
Jeera	Cumin seeds
Kadhai/Karahi	Wok
Kaju	Cashewnuts
Katori	Individual serving bowls resembling ramekins
Keema	Mince meat

Khumb	Mushrooms
Kishmish	Raisins
Magaz	Melon seeds
Maida	All purpose flour, Plain flour
Makai, Makki	Corn
Makhan	Butter
Matar	Peas
Moong phalli	Peanuts
Moti Illaichi	Black cardamom
Murg	Chicken
Mutton	Lamb
Nimbu	Lemon
Paalak	Spinach
Paneer	Home made cheese made by curdling milk with vinegar or lemon juice. Fresh home made ricotta cheese can be substituted
Paraat	A shallow mixing bowl made of metal, usually for kneading dough
Patta Gobhi	Cabbage
Phalli	Green beans
Poodina	Mint
Powdered sugar	Castor sugar
Prawns	Shrimps
Pyaz, pyaaz	Onions
Red Capsicum	Red bell peppers
Red Chilli Flakes	Red pepper flakes
Rind	Zest, peel thinly scraped of orange or lemon
Roti	Whole wheat, flat bread resembling tortillas
Saboot Kali mirch	Peppercorns
Saunf	Fennel
Sela Chaawal	Parboiled rice, which when cooked is not sticky at all
Shimla Mirch	Green bell peppers
Soda bicarb	Baking soda
Spring Onions	Green onions, Scallions
Suji	Semolina
Tamatar	Tomato
Tawa	Griddle
Til	Sesame seeds
Toned Milk	Milk with 1% fat content
White butter	Unsalted butter
Yellow Capsicum	Yellow bell peppers
Zeera	Cumin seeds

Coconut Custard : Recipe on page 89 ➢
Dates on Fire : Recipe on page 90 ➢

BEST SELLERS BY *Nita Mehta*

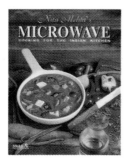

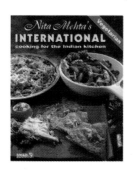

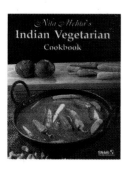

BEST SELLERS BY Nita Mehta

Nita Mehta's Simply Delicious CURRIES

RECIPES IN HINDI & ENGLISH

Nita Mehta's The Best of MICROWAVE Cooking
सर्वश्रेष्ठ माईक्रोवेव खाना

A BI-LINGUAL COOKBOOK

Nita Mehta's DELHI Ka KHAANA

Nita Mehta's Everyday Cooking
100% TRIED & TESTED RECIPES

Over 120 Vegetarian Delights

Nita Mehta's VEGETARIAN WONDERS
BEST SELLER
100% TRIED AND TESTED RECIPES

Nita Mehta's Perfect Vegetarian Cookery

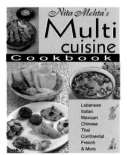

Nita Mehta's Multi cuisine Cookbook
Lebanese
Italian
Mexican
Chinese
Thai
Continental
French
& More

Nita Mehta's FOOD from around the WORLD

Nita Mehta's VEGETARIAN Snacks
100% TRIED & TESTED RECIPES

Nita Mehta's ITALIAN

100% TRIED AND TESTED RECIPES

Nita Mehta's CONTINENTAL Non-Vegetarian

Nita Mehta's The Best of MUTTON

THE BEST OF CHICKEN RECIPES

Nita Mehta's CHINESE cookery

Nita Mehta's Indian COOKING

Nita Mehta's Indian LOW FAT cookbook

LOW CALORIE RECIPES

Nita Mehta's Low Calorie SNACKS

Nita Mehta's Mexican Vegetarian Cookery

Nita Mehta's MICROWAVE Cookery
100% TRIED & TESTED RECIPES

Nita Mehta's Mocktails & Snacks

Nita Mehta's MORE DESSERTS